Acts of Faith

Also by Iyanla Vanzant

Iyanla Vanzant

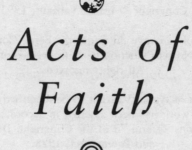

Acts of
Faith

DAILY MEDITATIONS
FOR PEOPLE OF COLOUR

POCKET
BOOKS

LONDON · SYDNEY · NEW YORK · TOKYO · SINGAPORE · TORONTO

First published in Great Britain by
Simon & Schuster UK Ltd, 1993
This edition first published by Pocket Books, 2004
An imprint of Simon & Schuster UK Ltd
A Viacom Company

1 3 5 7 9 10 8 6 4 2

Simon & Schuster UK Ltd
Africa House
64–78 Kingsway
London WC2B 6AH

www.simonsays.co.uk

Simon & Schuster Australia
Sydney

A CIP catalogue record for this book is available
from the British Library

ISBN 0-7434-8439-8

Typeset by Palimpsest Book Production Limited
Polmont, Stirlingshire

Printed and bound in Great Britain by
Bookmarque Ltd, Croydon, Surrey

For

My Father
Horace Lester Harris, all you were and all you were not;

My Brother
Horace Raymond Harris, Jr, all I needed you to be;

My Son
Damon Keith Vanzant, all you are;

My Grandson
Oluwalomoju Adeyemi, all you are becoming.

To the descendants of the Africans who long to know themselves: Although the days of glory may appear to be over, the spiritual heritage is everlasting. You must know with all your heart – It Doesn't Have To Be A Struggle!

May the Ancestors bless you with a clear mind, a peace-filled heart and a powerful African spirit.

OBATALA! Baba Mi, A'dupe.
Egun Ye.
(Translation: The Father of Creation,
My Father, I Salute You. Iyanla)

ACKNOWLEDGMENTS

My heartfelt appreciation, love and gratitude to my daughter *Gemmia* for her contribution to ten of these pages;

My daughter *Nisa* for stopping my grandson from eating these pages;

Ralph Stevenson for putting up with my endless requests and taking me anywhere and everywhere while I was in labour with this book;

Kim Mickens, who typed and retyped and never once complained when I scribbled changes on the pages she had just retyped;

Dawn Daniels, my editor, who supported and trusted me enough to know it had to be done;

Shaheerah Linda Beatty, who loved and prayed me through the entire process by making arrangements with Detroit Bell so we could stay in touch;

BarbaraO and *Nana Korantemaa*, who never asked me a question they could not answer;

My *Godfather*, who prayed the power down and sent it to my house;

My *Transformation Station* family in Philadelphia and Detroit, who never stopped praying, praising and pumping me up;

and, of course, God, who always knew I had it in me and finally convinced me, too.

PERMISSIONS

Heartfelt appreciation and humble recognition is given for permissions granted by the following:

Special thanks to all those quoted for their wisdom and the courage to share themselves with the world.

I will be found by you and I will bring you back from your captivity; I will gather you from all the nations and from all the places where I have driven you; And, I will bring you to the place from which I caused you to be carried away captive.

– Jeremiah 29:10–14

THE HEALING HAS BEGUN

It began when you picked up this book. The goal of these offerings is to assist the children of the earth in the redevelopment of their minds, bodies and spirits. Who are the children of the earth? The children of a darker hue. For they are the ones born of the first Father and Mother. They are the ones who learned, through trial and error, how to bring forth the abundant richness of the earth. They are the ones who have the secret of the beginning and the end buried deep in their souls. These offerings are tools to be used to dig up the secrets so that they can be put to use.

There are a few minor requirements to which one should adhere in order to realize the full value of these offerings. First, you must be open, ready and willing to receive the information. Some of it will be new to you. Most of it you have heard at some time, in some way. The difference is that now you are willing to see, hear and use the information to accomplish a goal: stress-free, peace-filled living. You must be willing to accept that stress is the result of unfinished business. Unfinished business means that there are details which have not been taken care of. Those details are the basic foundation of what you do. What you do is live, and life must begin within. That is the second requirement. The third and final requirement is the willingness to reevaluate, reprogramme and rechannel your thinking. Stress will not go away until you decide it no longer has a place in your Life. Obstacles and challenges will not stop until your perception of them changes. Difficulties and disappointments may not cease, yet you can see them in a different light, with a new sense of knowing; everything in life is purposeful.

There are four basic areas that create stress and imbalance for people of colour: our relationship with ourselves, our relationship with the world, our relationship with each other and our relationship with money. Consequently, this book has been divided into those four sections. Each will provide you with offerings to consider and hopefully put to use in restructuring your approach and perceptions. It does not matter who you are or where you are in any of those areas. You can make changes, realize improvement and eliminate stress in all of your relationships.

Take time to read a statement daily. Write or repeat the affirmation so that it will make an imprint on your mind. Forty is the number of building foundations. You might want to try repeating the affirmation forty times throughout the day. If you forget, four times will do as the number four represents the cardinal elements (air, water, fire, earth) and the cardinal directions (north, south, east, west). If you can't do that, reading a page a day will still have an effect, there is something for everyone.

Remember also, 'As a man soweth in his heart, so shall he reap.' What you put into the process of freeing your mind and life from stress, you will get out of it. Change is not easy. Yet it doesn't have to be difficult. A very dear astrologer friend of mine, Basil Farrington, once gave me a very good analysis of making change. I share it with you in the hope that it will assist you:

Buried deep in the earth are precious diamonds. In order to get to them, however, we must dig and dig deep. Once we get to the foundation rock, we must apply pressure to shape and mould the diamond. It is not the digging, it is the pressure that makes diamonds. Softness is what marshmallows are made of. Soft, sweet, easy to crumble under pressure and no good for anybody. You are being challenged to decide what you want to be – a diamond or a marshmallow – wait, I think I see a sparkle in your eye! The pressure is on, the healing has begun! May the glow from the sparkle in your eye bring light to all the world.

I SALUTE YOU

AND HONOUR YOUR GREATNESS

Iyanla

SELF

1 *January*

There is a power greater than myself who loves me exactly as I Am.

●

The stress began the day you learned you were expected to please other people. Parents wanted you to stay clean and be quiet. Neighbours wanted you to be respectful and helpful. Teachers wanted you to be attentive and alert. Friends wanted you to share and hang out. Whenever you failed to do exactly what someone expected of you, you weren't good, or good enough. You were bad, weak or dumb. Unfortunately, you began to believe it. Giving in to the demands, day by day, you lost a little more of yourself and your understanding of the truth. The truth is you are fine, just the way you are! Perfect in your imperfection! You are divine! Growing brighter and more brilliant each day, you can accept the truth of who you are. The next time you want to know who you are, what you are or if something is the right thing to do, don't ask your neighbour – ask the power within . . . and pay attention to the response!

The divine power within knows exactly who I Am!

2 January

Our hearts are the wrapping which preserve God's
word, we need no more.
– The Koran, Sura 4:155

●

When was the last time you sat down to have a heart
to heart with yourself? Have you really examined your
heart lately? Are you harbouring childhood wounds? Are
you still nursing a broken heart? Are you frightened?
Angry? Guilty or ashamed? Is there someone you need
to apologize to? Who have you forgiven lately? If God
were to speak through your heart today, what would you
hear? In the everyday quest to get through life, we sometimes forget we really do have all we need. It's tucked
away safely inside of us. It contributes to our thoughts
and motivates our actions. If we clear it out it will actually speak to us and tell us exactly what to do. When
was the last time you had a heart to heart with yourself?

With a pure heart, I am balanced in life.

3 *January*

Don't be afraid to look at your faults.
– Yoruba proverb

●

Even though we know there is always room for improvement, we tend to shy away from criticism. Our egos tell
us we are being attacked and quite naturally we want to
strike back. In order to be whole, healthy beings, we need
to know all there is to know about ourselves. Sometimes
that information must come from others. This may mean
admitting that we are not always right, and knowing it
is okay to make a mistake. A mistake, an error, a poor
choice or bad decision does not equal 'there is something
wrong with me'. It means you are on your way to being
better. We do not make mistakes on the basis of race or
colour. We make them because we are human. When we
acknowledge our errors and face up to our shortcomings,
no one can use them against us.

I Am not afraid to admit when I am wrong.

4 January

Take a day to heal from the lies you've told yourself
and the ones that have been told to you.
– Maya Angelou

●

There comes a time when we have to pause to listen
to what we are telling ourselves – 'I'm so stupid,' 'I'm
broke,' 'I don't know how,' 'I can't take it any more
. . .' Yet in the midst of our dishonest chatter we are
making great strides, accomplishing many tasks, over-
coming seemingly insurmountable odds. We can't see it
because we keep lying to ourselves. We lie because we've
been lied to – 'You're no good,' 'You can't do it,' 'You'll
never make it,' 'How do you think you're gonna do that
. . .' We can't think because there are so many lies running
loose in our minds. The only way to eradicate a lie is
with the truth. We must not only speak the truth, we
must think in truth. The truth is, we start from a place
where success is born, in the mind's eye of the Most High.
The truth is that no one has ever made a true deal with
the Master and lost.

The truth springs forth from my mind.

5 January

STOP!

●

Most of us know exactly what it is that creates the pain, confusion, stagnation and disruption in our lives. Whether it is a habit, behaviour, relationship or fear, we know. Unfortunately, we seem powerless to stop whatever it is. Sometimes we believe we don't have the discipline or willpower to stop. The behaviour becomes so habitual we do it without thinking. Other times we know exactly what it is and what we do, but we simply keep doing it anyway. We are the only ones responsible for what goes on in our lives. We can make excuses and blame others, but we are responsible to and for ourselves. When we find something or someone creating in our lives that which we do not want, we must muster the courage and strength to stop it.

Today I use my power to stop what is no longer good to me.

6 *January*

You've got to get the mind cleared out before you put
the truth in it.
– Minister Louis Farrakhan

●

Everyone has something they are ashamed of, afraid
of or that they feel guilty about. Each of us in our own
way will devise a neat little method of handling it. Some
of us deny. Some of us blame. Some of us do a combi-
nation of both. Undoubtedly the day will come when we
will be forced to examine that which we have tucked
away. We can willingly begin the process of examination
by telling the truth to ourselves about ourselves. We all
have the right to make mistakes. Our fault is being right-
eous about it. When we fail to admit our faults, the faults
become what everyone can see. When we refuse to admit
what we have done in the past, we block our path to the
future. No matter how terrible we think we are, how bad
we believe we have been, how low we think we have
fallen, we can clean out our minds and begin again.

The only way out is truth.

Do not wish to be anything but what you are, and to
be that perfectly.
– St François de Sales

●

A minister friend of mine once told me, 'On the seventh
day God rested.' He said, 'It is good and very good.'
Then we come along and try to improve on perfection.
For people of colour, the most damaging habit we have
is trying to be who and what we are not. We expend so
much energy trying to fix who we are, we rarely get to
really know ourselves. If we truly realized how precious
the gift of life is, we would not waste a moment trying
to improve it. If we really understood how precious we
are to the gift of life, we would not waste time trying to
fix ourselves. It's not about what we look like or what
we have. It's not about fixing our face, body or lives. It's
about taking what we have and doing as much as we can
with it. It's about learning and growing. When we are
willing to learn what we don't know and use our experiences, our perfection will begin to show.

I accept me as I Am.

8 January

Know thy ideal and live for that. For each soul must
give an account for its own self.
— Paramhansa Yogananda

●

Everything that happens to us, and every choice we
make, is a reflection of what we believe about ourselves.
We cannot outperform our level of self-esteem. We cannot
draw to ourselves more than we believe we are worth.
The things we believe and say about ourselves come back
to us in many ways. Self-motivation comes from self-
knowledge. We must inspire ourselves by believing we
have the power to accomplish everything we set out to
do. We must put faith in our ability to use mind and
spirit and picture our lives the way we want them to be.
We must use inner strength and the power of our being
to tear down the walls, break through the barriers and
move through the obstacles with ease. Our bodies have
been freed. Now we must train our minds to believe it.

I Am free, hallelujah, I Am free!

9 *January*

You may not know how to raise your self-esteem, but
you definitely know how to stop lowering it.
— Awo Osun Kunle

●

Self-esteem is a sense of value and worth that comes
from a positive self-image. Self-esteem begins with you
and extends to all that you do. With the belief that your
best is always good enough, no one but you can destroy
your self-esteem. You destroy your esteem when you do
not keep your word. When you do not honour the agreements and commitments you make. If you say 'yes' when
you really mean 'no'. When you don't follow your first
thought. It does not matter what your environment may
be. It is of little consequence what your past has been. It
is not your concern what others may be saying or doing.
It is only in your mind that you build and destroy your
self-esteem.

I Am as great as I think I Am.

10 January

It thy right eye offends thee, pluck it out . . .
– Matthew 5:29

●

The only way to eliminate stress and pain is to stop doing the things that create it. It is easy to see what others do to us while we forget the drama we create for ourselves. How? Take your pick: The need to be right. Lack of life purpose. How we think others see us. Trying to fix the world. Dishonesty with self and others. Accepting someone else's truth. Seeking material wealth over spiritual values. Doing it alone. My way is the right way. Fear of the future. Negative thought patterns. Trying to prove yourself to others. Anger over the past. Telling other people what to do. It all boils down to 'not knowing who we are'.

When I know me, I stop doing what's not good for me.

11 January

When you strengthen your self-esteem, there is no
room for jealousy.
– Dr Harold Bloomfield

●

Jealousy is the surest way to get rid of the very person
you are afraid of losing. When you say I love you, it
means 'I want the very best for you whether or not I am
included.' You must acknowledge any feelings of jealousy
to understand what they are. Jealousy is a signpost of the
longings in your subconscious mind. It reminds you that
what you are longing is also longing you. There are only
two emotions, love and fear. When jealousy comes up,
stop and recognize that it is actually fear raising its ugly
head. Fear of losing someone or something, fear that
there is not enough. If you allow yourself to be jealous,
you cannot love. It is important to acknowledge all your
feelings and not beat yourself up for having them. Your
feelings are not good or bad, they just are. Jealousy is
simply reminding you that you are worthy of the best.
When you remember who you are, the jealousy will
dissolve and you will be ready to receive what you want.

I honour my feelings no matter what they are.

12 January

There's absolutely no way to save people from the
things in their eyes. They must gather the courage to
do it for themselves.
— Alvin Lester Ben-Moring

●

Before we were indoctrinated to the rules of the world,
with all its do's and don'ts, we were actually very receptive. We were willing to try new things, go into forbidden
places and take risks without hesitation. We did not believe
in unhappiness, defeat, rejection or lack. We asked for
what we wanted and were willing to demand that it be
provided. We thought the world existed to respond to
our needs. It might do us well to revert back to the ways
of childhood if we want to bring some good into our
lives. It's not the temper tantrums or childish outbursts
we want. It is the openness and freedom from limitation
we need. We have been taught to accept fear, lack, sorrow
and restriction as a part of everyday life. We are afraid
to make demands of life because we believe we can't have
what we want. We no longer feel free to express what
we feel, when we feel it. Now, we want to be everyone's
friend. If only we could think like a child again, there's
a good chance we would find the freedom we gave up
to become adults.

Today, I Am a child again.

13 January

Heaven is where you'll be when you are okay right
where you are.
– Sun Ra

●

Pretend for a moment that you are a mink – beautiful,
valuable, precious because of the skin that covers you.
Suddenly your homeland is invaded by hunters, with bats.
The hunters seem kind, yet you approach them cautiously.
They pet the younglings who are innocent, less cautious.
As you approach your young, the hunters attack. They
beat you. You are dazed, struggling for composure. The
hunters steal your skin, your heritage, the very essence
of your being. They leave you to die, but you survive.
Your fur grows back. Stronger. More beautiful than before.
Somehow it doesn't make sense. The very thing that
makes you who and what you are is the source of pain.
Confused, distrustful, you hide yourself or camouflage
your fur, your essence. Silently you begin to curse your
fur, because the hunters return again and again. You begin
to understand you will never get away from being what
you are. As long as you have fur, you will be hunted.
The issue is: Will you curse your fur, give up and die?
Or just continue to be a proud but cautious mink?

I will not hide who or what I Am.

14 January

Successful people succeed because they learn from
their failures.
– Bettina Flores

●

The most difficult things to face in life are the things
you do not like about yourself. Not your ears, legs, hair
or those habits and abilities you feel are not up to par.
It is the ugly little things you know about yourself that
need a good long look. You recognize it when you see it
in others, but you make excuses for yourself. You may
go to any length to cover a shortcoming, while you
quickly point out the ills of another. Since the very thing
you want to hide is the thing that shows itself, you need
to be able to say, 'I know that and I'm working on it!'
It takes a loving heart, a willing mind and a sensitive
spirit to get to the core of the self. But when you do, you
can root out the seeds of ugliness.

I acknowledge, accept and embrace everything about me.

15 January

We [must] realize that our future lies chiefly in our
own hands.
– Paul Robeson

●

If you can blame anyone for any condition in your life,
then you, not they, are digging your grave. Your chief
adversary comes to teach you a lesson. Your most difficult challenge strengthens your survival skills. Your greatest
fear deepens your faith. Your weakest ability beckons you
to grow. Anyone and anything can challenge you. It will
not overtake you until you surrender. Only you can determine what you do and how you respond in a situation.
It is your responsibility to make a decision about what
is important to you; choose what you want and how you
are going to get it. Once you accomplish that, it is your
responsibility to move forward until you get it.

I Am taking a stand for me.

16 January

Sitting in a sacred place means you must sit alone.
– Marilyn 'Omi Funke' Torres

●

There are times when we each have sacred blessings to learn. These are the lessons that will push us to the limit of our greatness. At these times, it may seem that others are abandoning, rejecting or criticizing us without just cause. They are not. No matter how hard we try, we can't seem to do, say or be what others expect of us. We can't. The harder we try to pull others to us, the farther they move away. The more we try to fix things, the worse they seem to get. What we must do at these very sacred times is pull back, withdraw and prepare to grow. Our lessons are very sacred. They are the basic ingredient of our greatness. To accept them we must be open. To receive them we must be willing. To understand them we must be alone.

I Am sitting in a sacred place.

17 January

In the solitude of your mind are the answers to all your questions about life. You must take the time to ask and listen.
– Bawa Mahaiyaddeen

●

There are times when we all feel as if we need to be alone. We just want to get away from everyone and everything and be alone. Sometimes we may feel guilty or selfish for thinking this way, but it is perfectly normal. To be alone is the best thing we can do for ourselves. To be alone means to be all one with the spirit within. When we are alone, we have an opportunity to get in touch with, to talk to and be guided by our power source. Spirit. To be alone means going to the essence of your being. To ask questions within and get clear, concise answers. To be alone means taking the time to give to yourself a small portion of what we have been giving of ourselves for so long. It is like drinking from the fountain of restoration to bring back your physical, mental and spiritual health. So go ahead. Tell them all and don't feel bad about saying it. 'I want to be alone.'

Today I Am all one with the spirit within.

18 January

I have never been contained except that
I made the prison.
– Mari Evans

●

When you concern yourself with doing only what others 'think' you can do, you lay the floor of your prison. When you conform your activities based on what others might say, you put the bars around your prison. When you allow what others have done or are doing to determine what you can do, you build the roof of your prison. When you allow fear, competition or greed to guide your actions, you lock yourself up and throw away the key. It is our concern over what others say, do and think about us that imprisons our mind, body and spirit.

What other people think about me is not my concern.

19 January

In our deepest hour of need the Creator asks
for no credentials.
– Eulogy of Horace Harris

●

There are times when we feel bad about ourselves, what we've done and what we are facing. In these moments we may even believe we deserve to be punished, because we are 'bad' or have done bad things. There are times when we feel so low, we convince ourselves that we don't matter and neither does anything or anyone else. That is when we usually start to think about God. Is there such a thing? Does God really care? Maybe if we had gone to God before, we wouldn't be where we are now. No matter. We're here, so let's go. This is a prime opportunity to make a new start, begin again and move on. The key is to remember that no matter where we've been, what we've done or how awful we feel right now, the One we may be running from knows exactly where we are. He has placed a light of peace in our hearts. A prayer will flip the switch.

I look within for all the answers I need.

You must learn how to make it on the broken pieces.
– Rev. Louise Williams-Bishop

●

Ripped from their land; stripped of their culture, religion, name; beaten for rebelling and blamed for their state of existence, the descendants of the Africans have a right to feel broken. Being broken does not mean you are unequipped. There are enough pieces left for you to grab on to, hold on to and paddle your way to shore. Your life is the piece that equips you to have a goal. Your goal is the piece that will equip you with confidence. Your confidence is the piece that will give you persistence. Your persistence is the piece that will ensure your success. There are pieces from your parents, friends, even foes. There are pieces of books, songs and experience. More important, there are the pieces that well up from deep inside your being that will guide you surely and safely. Put them all together and hold on.

My pieces may be broken but I am going on anyhow.
– Rev. Louise Williams-Bishop

21 January

You are as much as you are right now.
– Yoruba proverb

●

We have such poor images of ourselves that we have difficulty understanding the good others see in us. When someone gives us a compliment, we are quick to point out what is wrong. When someone supports or encourages us, we remind them of our failures. We play ourselves down to such a degree that others begin to question the faith they have placed in us. This vicious cycle can only lower our already low self-esteem. Today is a good time to rethink our thoughts about ourselves. We can accept the compliments we receive when we give them to ourselves first. We can build our confidence by celebrating our small victories and successes. We can support the faith and trust others have in us by supporting and having faith in ourselves. It all begins with our willingness to acknowledge that we are really fine, just the way we are.

I really am okay with me.

22 January

God isn't alarmed when we hit rock bottom. He made
the rock.
– Baptist Minister

●

There are times in our lives when we feel there is no
way up or out. Illness. Poverty. Confusion. Loneliness.
Desperation. They take us to the place called 'rock bottom'.
In these times you may feel weak and vulnerable, and it
is easy to lose faith in your ability to go on. It is exactly
in these times that you must turn to the infinite power
within yourself. You must know that the answer is exactly
where you are. The strength you need, the answer you
want, the solution that will turn the situation around is
you. If you can put aside the anger, fear, weakness and
desperation for just a minute you will remember the
'other times' you were at the bottom and how in a moment,
miraculously, you were lifted up.

There is no spot where God is not.

23 January

Ask, and it shall be given you . . .
— Matthew 7:7

●

We all get to a point where we feel confused and inde-
cisive. We can't seem to figure out what we want or what
to do. We want everything, but nothing brings satisfac-
tion. Our spirit is restless because the mind is racing. It
may not be that we don't know, it is probably that we
are afraid to ask. We may feel as if we are running to
something, but actually we are running away. In those
times we need to sit down, get still and evaluate just what
it is we want. We must do this quietly, honestly and often,
if necessary. We are human beings, blessed with the power
of reason. We have, at all times, the right and the power
to figure out what we want. Once that's done, we must
have the courage to ask for it. If we let the colour of our
skin, the gender we express or the ways of the world limit
us, we will forever be denied. We owe it to ourselves to
choose a way and ask for it. Once we ask, we can rest.

Today I plan to choose and ask with an open mind.

24 January

For no man can be blessed without the acceptance of
his own head.
— Yoruba proverb

●

The wise Africans knew and understood the power of
the mind. People can only be as good as their thoughts,
as successful as mental patterns, as progressive as their
ideas. Africans did not rely on books, relative theories or
postulative quotations. They listened to their thoughts,
prayed for divine guidance, followed the intuitive urging.
Education, money, fame and notoriety were considered as
useful as dirty dishwater without a clear, firm, focused
mind. Their process was simple. They developed a strong
faith and connection to the Creator. A healthy love and
respect for their ancestors and parents. A commitment and
dedication to the traditions of their family. And a trusting
relationship to the spirit of their own head. Trust your
head and your first thought regardless of what others may
say. Your head takes you to the places you want to go.

I bless the spirit of my head.

25 January

Check out your own B.S.
– Jewel Diamond-Taylor

●

B.S. refers to Belief System – those things you hold to be true about yourself and others. Your B.S. is a product of your experiences and perceptions. Those things you have come to believe are true. Those things buried in the back of your mind. But are they really buried? *No!* Your belief system determines your environment, your abilities and the way you approach life's experiences. What do you really believe about yourself? What do you believe about your ability to have, to be and to do all the things you hold dear in your heart? If you really want to know what you believe, take a look at the people, conditions and situations in your immediate environment. They are the reflection of your own B.S.

I Am a true believer in the best about me.

26 January

It takes a deep commitment to change and an even
deeper commitment to grow.
– Ralph Ellison

●

When you know you are thinking, saying or doing
things that are unhealthy or unproductive, you must do
more than know. There must be a genuine, loving support
for the 'self' to make a change. Change does not mean
replacing one bad habit for another. It does not mean
beating up on yourself or feeling guilty or ashamed. Change
means voluntarily removing yourself from the people and
environment that support you in remaining unhealthy.
Change means identifying what you are doing, recognizing when you are doing it and gently guiding yourself
to do something else. Change means not making excuses
for yourself, but doing exactly what you say you will do.
When you support yourself in making needed changes,
you are supporting your own growth. Growth is the
commitment to being, doing and having the best.

I Am growing by thoughts, words and deeds.

27 January

There are two things over which you have complete
dominion, authority and control – your mind and
your mouth.
– Molefi Asante

●

Your mind is an instrument. A precious gift to be
valued and cared for. You are not always in control of
what goes into your mind, but only you can determine
what stays there. If you allow negativity to pervade in
your mind, you will produce that negativity with your
mouth. Your mouth is the mechanism that reveals how
well you care for your mind. The conditions in your life
stem from the most dominant thoughts of which you
speak. Nothing has a hold on your mind that you cannot
break free of. Since your mind will respond to what is
said to you, speak to the conditions in your life. When
they are wanted, give thanks. When they are unwanted,
demand they change.

I Am in control of my mind and mouth.

28 January

You've got the right one, baby! Uh-huh!
– As performed by Ray Charles

●

You are the only one who can do it like you do it. You are the best. You have what it takes. You've got juice. You've got the power. You and only you have what you have, and nobody can take that away from you. You come from the best, the beginning, the source. You are destined to be great. You inherited a legacy of success from those who came before you. They knew you could do it, too! You are the light in life. You light up the world. You make life worth living. You can't lose with the stuff you use. You are the beginning and the end of the phenomenon called you. You are the one who makes the bed. You call the shots. You stand heads above the crowd. They can't hold a candle to you. When you put your mind to something, you get it done. So what are you waiting for?

I Am the you that can do it.

29 January

If you don't sell your head, no one will buy it.
– Yoruba proverb

●

We are capable of directing and determining the outcome of any and every situation we face through the power of thought. Yet since many of us do not realize our true power, we cannot realize the truth of the statement: 'No one can do anything or make you do anything unless you let them.' The key is to be honest with yourself and others at all times, keep your thoughts focused on the best possible outcome for everyone involved and never allow yourself to be pushed where you don't choose to be. If someone called you a grape, you probably wouldn't respond. But if that same person refers to you as a coon or spade, you would most likely hold them responsible for your reaction. No one but you can ever be held accountable for what you do. How you respond in any given situation is purely a reflection of what you think – what is in your head. When someone does or says something you believe is offensive, do yourself a favour – don't sell your head.

It's what's inside my head that counts.

30 January

Ford got a better idea, you can get one too.
– Linda Green Beatty

●

The things our parents tell us, the things we read in books, the things we hear and overhear create the foundation of our thoughts. These thoughts grow into ideas. For many people of colour, the ideas they have about themselves are not good. There is the idea that it is hard for Black people to make it. This is supported by the idea that Black people don't try. There is the idea that other people are preferred over Black people. This gives birth to the idea that Black people are not good enough. There is the idea that Black men aren't respected. This comes from the idea that Black women have abandoned Black men. The idea is that because there is so much conflict between Black men and Black women, Black children are lost. The thing we seem to forget is that an idea will die unless it is acted upon. Every time we entertain the truth of false ideas we give it the right to live. If an idea is not of your making or liking, you can choose to have a better one.

I believe in my right to have unlimited goodness in my life.

31 January

The mind is and always will be our primary business.
— Dr Benjamin Mays

●

There are times when it is difficult to make sense of the experiences we have in life. How are we to get ahead without money? How are we to overcome intangible obstacles? How are we to move through the challenges, difficulties and limitations we face at every turn? It may seem that no matter how hard you try, something or someone is there to block you. In those times remember the words of Dr Benjamin Mays:

It is not your environment;
It is not your history;
It is not your education or ability;
It is the quality of your mind that predicts your future.

I take the time to develop my own mind.

1 *February*

Even if you're on the right track, you'll get run over if
you just sit there.
– Will Rogers

●

A positive, healthy sense of self-value and worth is the
foundation of our happiness and success. When we know
who we are and believe it, our greatest dreams are possible.
When we doubt ourselves, question our worth, and under-
mine our self-value, our greatest victory will be worthless. Affirm 'I am my greatest hero.' That is really where
it starts. We must believe in who we are and what we
do. We must look up to and trust ourselves to make it
through the difficulties knowing that we can. Only we
can truly appreciate and celebrate our own success. We
are equipped and capable of getting to where we want
to be. If we have any doubts, we can always hold our
own hand.

*I now create a positive pattern of self-worth because I
believe I Am the best.*

2 *February*

If you plant turnips you will not harvest grapes.
– Akan proverb

●

When we pass a garden and see everything in full bloom, we don't always think about the seeds that were planted long before we got there. We simply enjoy the beauty of the harvest. Our minds work the very same way. It is the law of expression that says we must ultimately express in form those thoughts, emotions and impulses we store in the subconscious mind. That part of us does not think. It does not reason, balance, judge or reject. It is the fertile ground that accepts any and everything we plant. Good or evil, constructive or destructive, our lives will bear the fruit of the seeds we plant in our minds. If we have no faith, purpose or belief in ourselves, we cannot blame the world. We plant the roses or weeds we see in the garden. We can imagine good big things as well as troubling little things, our minds will accept either one. If we want to lay back and sniff the lilies in our valley, we must tend our seeds of thought with constant care.

I reap a good harvest from the soil of my mind.

3 *February*

The most sacred place isn't the Church, the Mosque or the Temple, it's the temple of the body. That's where spirit lives.
– Susan Taylor

●

Take a moment to check in on your body. Deeply inhale and exhale. Let your mind flow through your body. Check in on your feet, legs, hips. Let your mind roam your abdomen, your chest, your back. Scan your neck, shoulders, arms. What are you feeling? Fear, exhaustion, tension, anxiety, anger, guilt, shame? Inhale and exhale. Where are you feeling it? Legs? Back? Neck? Chest? Wherever it is, whatever it is, you are the only mechanic who can fine-tune your body. With a simple breath you can release the stress and replace it with what you need. Turn anxiety into peace, anger into joy, tension into love, fear into faith, guilt into trust. Take a moment right now and give yourself a tune-up.

When I am in tune with my body, I relax and release the stress.

4 February

May I assume whatever form I want in whatever space
my spirit wishes to be.
– *The Book of Coming Forth by Day*,
translated by Dr Maulana Karenga

●

The ancients knew the connection between man and
the Divine. They knew that buried beneath the personality, perceptions and self-imposed limitations there lies
a spirit of unlimited possibility. They knew that you choose
with your thoughts the shape and form of your life. You
create with your words the conditions that you will face.
You limit with your fear the coming forth of your desires.
You destroy with your blame the direction of your destiny.
The ancient ones knew that only with diligent maintenance of the mind and emotions would man master his
fate. Because the blood of the ancient ones runs through
your veins, you have the same knowledge. You have the
ability to be what you want in the place you may choose.
Simply follow the divine prescription for unfettered success,
'Begin within.'

I Am the beginning and my end.

5 February

Nothing can dim the light which shines from within.
– Maya Angelou

●

Each of us brings to the world unique talents, gifts and abilities. Even if you don't know what it is, or value what you do, someone, somewhere, will benefit from your presence. No one can do what you do exactly the way you do it. It is this uniqueness that makes you valuable to the world. We are each as unique and valuable as the other. It was designed that way. A gift from God. Gifts are not given on the basis of race or gender. As a matter of truth, gifts come in many shapes, sizes and colours. When you do what you do, exactly the way you do it, you are sharing God's gifts, bestowed for the good of the world.

I have something valuable to give the world.

6 February

Nobody knows the mysteries which lie at the bottom
of the ocean.
– Yoruba proverb

●

Your body is 96 percent water. Like the ocean, you are
a mystery of buried treasures. The deeper you are willing
to go, the greater are the treasures you will find. Your
mind is the only equipment you need. The sharper your
mind, the greater the depths that will be revealed to you.
Never allow anyone or anything to limit your mind because
of your race, colour or gender expression, since your
mind feeds your emotions. The emotions of your heart
will keep your dreams afloat. If you can feel it, the world
must reveal it. When you take time to breathe consciously,
stilling the motion of the mind, you can take a plunge
into the deepest resources of your soul. Take a plunge
within yourself to find the joy, strength, peace, freedom
and love you may be seeking in the shores of life.

*I look within the ocean of self to find
the treasures of life.*

7 February

If you have no confidence in self, you are twice defeated in the race of life. With confidence, you have won even before you have started.
– Marcus Garvey

●

A history of oppression, denial, injustice and abuse has been the greatest detriment to people of colour. We have listened so long to what we cannot do that we have very little confidence in what we can do. It is this lack of confidence, not racism, hatred, lack of education or social injustice that creates the greatest deterrent to our progress. One of the best-kept secrets in life is when children of God make up their minds, when they bring their minds into harmony with the desire in their hearts, when they pray for and follow intuitive guidance; then no one and nothing can stop them – no matter what colour they may be. Confidence and a made-up mind are the stuff kings and queens are made of.

I Am confident and possess all I need to succeed.

8 February

Luck is what happens when preparation
meets opportunity.
– Unknown

●

Fear, lack of confidence and low self-esteem tend to make us jump to conclusions. If what we are facing is near to our hearts, we have a tendency to expect the worst. We miss so much, including opportunities to change, when we jump to the end from the middle. We forget our focus and the goal when we poise ourselves for failure. The ancient Africans knew that no matter what was going to happen, it would not happen until it happened. Therefore, they were prepared for all possibilities, the good and the bad. Do not jump to conclusions, you could be wrong. Do not pull out in the middle, that is a total waste of time. Keep your faith, trust and stay focused, put your best foot out anyway. The ancient ones had faith and trusted, knowing the end is only a reflection of the beginning.

The end is not here yet.

I am sick and tired of being sick and tired.
– Fannie Lou Hamer

●

Many of us believe that unless we are struggling, we are not doing it right. We struggle with thoughts, feelings, even other people. We struggle with money problems, family problems and personal problems. Many of us have said, 'I am tired of struggling!' Well, guess what? When you make the decision to stop struggling, you will stop. When you stop struggling, things get better. Struggle goes against the flow. It creates exhaustion in the mind and body. When you are exhausted you get sick. If you are sick, you must make a decision and commitment to do everything in your power to get better. The power is in the commitment never to do what makes you sick. The key is the decision never to tire of doing what is best, good and right for you.

I give no thing power over me.

10 February

There must be inner healing for the broken vessels.
– Rev. Linda Hollies

●

She spent two days making her outfit, spent her last $50 on a new pair of shoes. She had her hair and nails done, spent forty-five minutes putting on her make-up. When she got there, she spent the entire evening sitting in the corner, half smiling, half crying. On the outside she looked beautiful. On the inside she felt worthless. So many of us invest a fortune making ourselves look good to the world, yet on the inside we are falling apart. We manage to muddle through life saying and doing the right things, but when we're alone we cry silent and desperate tears. It is time to pause and heal the inside. It is time to heal the hurts, mend the fences, dig up the hatchets and throw them away. It is time to heal the doubts, answer the questions and release the fears. It is time to invest some time to what is going on inside. When we can do that, the outside will shine.

I Am investing my time in something that matters.

11 February

When there's anger in your head, rage in your heart,
that's the time you can't forget to boogie!
– BarbaraO

●

Many people of colour are extremely diverse, wonderfully creative and desperately depressed. For some reason, all we know, are capable of doing and desire to accomplish never gets done. We seem to be held down by our frustrations, challenges and failures. This in turn makes us so angry we could scream. What we fail to realize is that anger is what stops us in the first place. It's not the other way around. Angry people are stagnant. Angry people are frustrated. Angry people see challenges as obstacles. Angry people fail before they start so they usually never try. Angry people tell themselves, 'I'm not angry, I'm Black. I'm not angry, I'm poor. I'm not angry, I'm just tired.' Yet buried beneath the poverty and fatigue is the black hole of anger that must be healed. Anger, not depression. Anger, not alcoholism. Anger, not hypertension. Anger, not cancer. Anger, not strokes is what holds us back, so we might as well scream and let a little of the anger out.

I Am willing to recognize and address anger when I experience it.

12 February

Depression is anger that you turn on yourself.
– Dr Craig K. Polite

●

There is a collective pain among people of colour that has been denied, mislabelled or unacknowledged. The pain of our collective past, the pain of our parents, the pain we experienced as children, the pain we create for one another. Regardless of the source or the age of the wounds, our pain is the source of our anger. Yet we are taught it is not 'nice' to be angry. We are discouraged from voicing or acting out on what we feel. We come up with cute little names for the things we do to deny that we are angry. When we fail to acknowledge anger, it quickly becomes depression and the weight makes it difficult to move forward. It robs us of our dreams. It steals precious hours, days and years. Depression may be labelled laziness, confusion, ignorance or just the way we are. Very often these labels make us angry. The only way to end the cycle and get off the roller-coaster of denied emotions is to admit that we are angry and go within to find the remedy.

I Am angry and I Am still okay.

13 February

Don't worry, be happy.
– Bobby McFerrin

●

Worry is the vampire that drains life of its force. Worry stagnates the mind, creates an imbalance in the immune system; weakens the throat, your power and authority centre; impairs the ability to see beyond the thing being worried about. We worry about things we cannot control. We worry about the past and the future. We worry about those things we cannot do or have not done and how they will affect what we are doing right now. We worry about what we do not have, cannot get and things we have lost. Worry creates confusion, disorder and help- lessness. Then we worry because we cannot figure things out. We must eliminate the tendency to worry without worrying if it will work out. Take the situation creating the worry, briefly and concisely write it down. Place the paper on which you have written in a window, facing the sun. Make a commitment to yourself to let it go and move on. Everyone knows that when sunlight hits a vampire, it first shrivels up and then it is gone.

I Am worry free.

14 *February*

Before you run, check to see if the bulldog has teeth.
– Les Brown

●

Fear is a very natural and normal response to the challenges we face in life. Fear tells us there is something we must be cautious about. Fear puts us on alert and tells us there is something we must be prepared for. Fear means something we know nothing about is about to come upon us. Fear of change, the unknown, rejection, failure and success are like the barking of a ferocious bulldog. For people of colour, the fear of being bitten, again, immobilizes us. A history that has not honoured our sense of worth and value supports the fear. The best thing we can do to fear is confront it. We must know the validity of the things we fear. We must believe we can conquer them. The next time the bulldog of fear is upon you, stare it down, open its mouth and check to see if the thing has teeth.

I give no power to fear.

15 February

A delay is not a denial.
– Rev. James Cleveland

●

Patience is a virtue many do not possess. We have very little difficulty identifying what we want and need. The difficulty comes in waiting for it to manifest. We become nervous, doubtful, even fearful when we don't see our good coming as quickly as we think it should. Sometimes we even allow ourselves to believe someone or something can hold us back or stop our good from coming. We worry, we complain and sometimes we give up hope. We cannot see how we get in our own way. We forget about universal timing and divine order. We may not realize how our negative thoughts, doubts and fears uproot the positive seeds we plant. We just don't understand that we would not have the desire unless the supply were ready to come forward. We must learn the virtue of patience because every time we open the oven door, we run the risk of making a good cake collapse.

I have all the time in the universe.

Keep thy heart with all diligence; for out of it are the
issues of life.
– Proverbs 4:23, 24

●

Queen Maat is the gatekeeper of the heart. It is said
that before man can pass on to eternal peace, his heart
must be balanced on the scale of Maat. On one side she
will place your heart, the cause behind all of your actions.
On the other side, she will place her feather, which contains
all the issues of life. If your heart tips the scale, you are
banished from a peaceful rest and your spirit must continue
working to cleanse itself. What are you harbouring in
your heart? Hate, anger, fear, judgment, shame or guilt
will tilt the scale against you. The feather of Maat contains
truth, honour, justice, harmony and love, which the
ancients believed were the only requirements for a long,
prosperous and peace-filled life. To pass through the gate
of Maat you must seek and speak the truth, harbouring
no ill thoughts or feelings, you must honour the ways of
those who came before you, you must deal justly with
honesty in all situations, be harmonious in all that you
do, seeking no quarrel with anyone and extending only
love to others.

My heart is as light as a feather.

17 February

I ain't gonna study war no more . . .
– African-American spiritual

●

Let us insist on peace today, turning our minds away from war. There is war in our hearts, minds, body organs and words because of the fast pace in which we live. Yet just for today, we will lay down our weapons, insisting that peace be the light and the way. Let us know today that we are spiritual beings, programmed for peace and love. Let us teach by example, demonstrating peace in everything we say and do. Let us know that it does not matter what others say or do. We will think in peace, speak in peace, knowing in our hearts that like will draw like. Let us know we are bound to become that which we study, so let us study peace and love and truth. If we commit ourselves to just one day of peace it is bound to feel so good, we will want to do it again.

I Am a peaceful warrior.

18 February

Don't let anyone steal your spirit.
– Sinbad

●

There are times when we find ourselves at odds with someone. It may seem that our only choices are to get caught up in the situation or walk away. The ego tells us we must prove we are right. If we walk away, the other person will win. The ego keeps us from recognizing there is another choice. Whatever situation confronts us, we must recognize our right to be at peace. The need to be right and meet discord head on begins within. It is a need that stems from feelings of powerlessness, unworthiness and a lack of love. It shows up in life as arguments and confrontation. When we have peace in our hearts and minds, we draw peace into our lives. When discord and disharmony present themselves, we can stand firm. When we let go of the need to prove to ourselves, nothing and no one can disturb the quiet and peace of our minds.

I Am rightfully peaceful.

19 February

Where you will sit when you are old shows where
you stood in youth.
– Yoruba proverb

●

We can become so consumed with trying to make it that we never do. Unfortunately, before we know it, we are seated by age, hardened by experiences, having never realized the full value of life. We want so much. We try to do so much, it seems as if nothing ever gets done. The ancient Africans knew that quality not quantity makes life precious. It is our individual responsibility to set the standards for quality in our lives. Do we have peace in our lives? Do we have a source of happiness in our lives? Are we living up to the standards we set for ourselves? Have we set standards? Are we committed to following our heart's desire? Are we making our dreams come true? We must decide for ourselves what we want for ourselves while the sunshine of youth is upon us. It is quality, not quantity, that brings wisdom with age.

I will let the sun of life shine on me.

20 February

You can look ahead, you can look behind, what is
written cannot be changed.
– *The Oracles of Ifa*

●

We cannot change the colour of our skin. What we
can change is how we feel about it. We cannot change a
pain-filled past. What we can do is change how it affects
us. We cannot change how others may feel about who
we are and where we've been. What we can change is
how we see it, how we use it and how others use it to
our benefit or detriment. The past has already been written,
but we have the power to write the future, based on who
we are and what we do now. Only we can write a future
based on self-support and respect. We can write a future
based on how much we have grown. We can write a
future full of strength, peace, wealth and love. All we
have to do is what is right now.

I Am choosing my future by what I do now.

21 February

Those whom the Gods would destroy, they
first call 'promising'.
– Jan Carew

●

The road of life is strewn with the bodies of promising
people. People who show promise, yet lack the confidence
to act. People who make promises they are unable to
keep. People who promise to do tomorrow what they
could do today. Promising young stars, athletes, entre-
preneurs who wait for promises to come true. Promise
without a goal and a plan is like a barren cow. You know
what she could do if she could do it, but she can't. Turn
your promise into a plan. Make no promise for tomorrow
if you are able to keep it today. And if someone calls you
promising, know that you are not doing enough today.

My life needs a plan not a promise.

22 February

Deal with yourself as an individual worthy of respect and make everyone else deal with you the same way.
– Nikki Giovanni

●

Many of us live from day to day without a real sense of purpose. We know we want more out of life, but we can't seem to put a finger on exactly what it is. We believe our fate is due to a lack of career, money or the freedom to do what we want. Actually, what we may be longing for is a personal mission. When you have a mission, you have a core passion that gives you vision. With the vision of your mission, you move gracefully through your goals. When you have a mission, you wholeheartedly embrace a task and you remain focused until the task is done. When you have a mission, you feel valued, worthy and respectable. You manage to keep your head up and others notice you. What is your mission? Is it teaching, healing, painting, driving? Perhaps it is building snowmen, counting pea pods or keeping others on their mission. Respect your life enough to pursue a meaningful mission. Respect yourself enough to give yourself something to do.

I Am mission-minded and focused on a goal.

23 February

The one thing grander than the sea is the sky.
The one thing greater than the sky is the spirit of the
human being.
– Anonymous

●

The reason we can't get clear is because we have so many things cluttering our minds and lives. We have so much mental chatter we can't hear ourselves think. We have so much emotional baggage we can't feel what's good, what's bad, what's right or what's wrong. We want so much, so fast, that we can't get clear about what to do first. The first thing we have to do is get clear about the one thing we want. We must describe it, identify it, see it in our possession. Don't stop to worry about how, that will create more clutter. Just want it and see it the way you want it. Once you do that, eliminate everything that is not getting you to what you want. Eliminate it from thought, word and deed. Eliminate people if necessary. Stop doing things that will not get you what you want. When you are comfortable with the energy you have put into your first want, move on to the next one. The trick is to want one thing at a time. Focus on it. Concentrate on it and then let it go.

I Am clear about what I want.
I can see through to it.

24 February

You must never be stupid enough to say, or smart
enough to admit, you 'know' what someone else is
talking about. The moment you do your learning stops.
– Awo Osun Kunle

●

The ego encourages you to constantly prove yourself
and what you already know. When you are in the presence of someone you feel the need to impress, the ego's
automatic response is 'I know'. When you are in the presence of someone your ego thinks is smarter, richer, more
experienced than you, your ego tells you, 'I know what
they are thinking about me.' When you are in the presence of someone your ego believes is not as smart, rich
or experienced as you, 'I know' is the way to cut them
off. The moment you say 'I know', you are demonstrating
that you don't know. You can learn something valuable
from everyone, in every situation.

I Am open and willing to learn.

25 February

Speak your truth and speak it quick!
– Michael Cornelius

●

Saying what you really think, feel or believe is often difficult. Usually you don't want to hurt other people's feelings. Even when they infuriate you, you don't want to make someone mad. The real truth of the matter is, somewhere deep down inside, you don't believe your feelings are 'right' or that you have the 'right' to feel the way you do. When you hold on to feelings you become angry, fearful and confused. When you don't say what is on your mind you will be prone to gossip, rebel or commit acts of betrayal against yourself and others. The only way to free yourself from the stress of not saying what you think is to speak your truth with love, clarity and conviction. And to speak it quickly with a conscious tongue.

I speak my truth from my heart.

26 February

You've been tricked! You've been had!
Hoodwinked! Bamboozled!
– El-Hajj Malik El-Shabazz (Malcolm X)

●

Somebody sure pulled a fast one on you! Somebody, somewhere tricked you into believing there were certain things you could not do because of who you were. Someone else told you that only certain people could do or be the very thing you wanted to be. And you were not one of those people. With a sleight-of-hand manipulation of facts, someone made you think you didn't have what it takes, so they took it. Somebody told you that you were slow, or lazy; not good enough; or crazy. And you believed that? They tricked you into believing what they wanted you to believe. They knew who you were and they knew you had no idea. They pulled the wool over your eyes. Ran a game on you and you fell for it! The truth is they downright, open-mouthed, bare-faced told you a lie! Now what are you going to do?

I am not falling for the same old tricks again.

27 February

The tongue of a man is his sword.
– *The Husia*, translated by Dr Maulana Karenga

●

Wars do not begin when one force is aggressive toward another. They begin when one force speaks aggression toward another. No act of aggression begins without a word. The word ignites the warrior mechanism in the mind and body. When we hear aggressive words, we are compelled to respond. When we speak aggressive words, we are advanced upon. A wise soldier knows never to draw his sword unless he is ready, able and willing to do battle. A fool draws his sword aimlessly and is prone to cut himself to death.

My tongue is my sword of power. I use it wisely.

28 February

You don't always have to have something to say.
– Sammy Davis, Jr

●

Every time we open our mouths we release a powerful energy. If we could learn to hold on to that energy, it could be used to nurture our dreams, heal our bodies and fuel our minds. But we always have so much to say. Talking can take us off the track, knock us off our centre and kill off our dreams when we speak mindlessly. Talking is something we must learn to use, not something we must always do. There is a power in silence that energizes the mind, body and soul. Think of the sun, moon and stars. They all appear silent and never fail at their job. There is wisdom in silence. Think of the mountains and trees. They never have anything to say, yet it takes great effort to bring them down. There is love in silence. Think of the womb. Perfect timing, order and completion accomplished in total silence. Silence is an art, a tool of the wise. When we perfect the art of silence, chances are we will get a lot more done.

Today I will practise the art of silence.

29 February

The dog is sometimes smarter than the owner.
– Yoruba proverb

●

The tongue has no mind of its own. Like a dog, the tongue follows where the owner leads. If the owner leads the dog into harm's way, the dog will not question the direction or intent. The same is true for the tongue. Unlike the dog, however, the tongue has a power the owner may not always be aware of. The tongue can create. The intent of the mind creates a force for the tongue. The power of this force will materialize as a physical condition or an emotional state for the owner. The tongue knows, even when the owner forgets, what you say is what you get – whether you want it or not.

I speak with a conscious tongue.

1 *March*

It is impossible to pretend that you are not heir to,
and therefore, however inadequately or unwillingly,
responsible to, and for, the time and place that
give you life.
– James Baldwin

●

We each come into this life to learn, relearn or unlearn
something we need to know. As difficult as it may be to
accept, we choose the exact circumstances into which we
are born. Whether it is poverty, abandonment, abuse,
rejection or disease, our deepest self knows the lessons
we must learn. Our mind chooses the path. Life's lessons
are few: peace, freedom, strength, justice, faith and love.
All the answers you need are buried within you. For just
a moment let go of the anger, fear, guilt, shame and
blame. Focus all of your attention on the centre of your
being and ask yourself, 'What is it that I must learn?'
The longer you ask, the more sincere you are to know,
the faster your answers will come.

I Am willing to take full responsibility for me.

2 March

Lord, make me so uncomfortable that I will do the
very thing I fear.
– Ruby Dee

●

When it is time for us to grow we get restless. When
it is time for us to move forward we get tense. When the
time comes for us to let go of the things we know are
holding us back, all hell breaks loose. Unfortunately, we
sometimes misunderstand what we are feeling and use it
as a reason to stay where we are. Nothing forces us to
move faster than pain. Restlessness is pain. Tension is
pain. Hell breaking loose is a sign that pain is on the
way. When we are in pain we must do something to make
ourselves feel better. And if the old remedy does not work,
we must try something new. Too many times we have cut
ourselves down to fit into the situation. Fixing ourselves
to stay where we are is the very source of our pain. If
we allow ourselves to live with a constant, dull ache, it
means we are not getting the message. But you can be
sure all dull aches eventually turn into a throbbing pain.

Pain tells me there is something wrong.

3 March

How I wish I could pigeon-hole myself and neatly fix a label on! But self-knowledge comes too late! By the time I've known myself I am no longer what I was.
– Mabel Segun

●

You are growing and learning every moment of every day. Regardless of what you have been told, you can and do change with every new experience. Each experience enhances your capabilities by giving you something new to draw upon. Every new capability you discover and develop leads to a new opportunity. As long as you have the capability and an opportunity, there is a new possibility for you to grow and learn something new. Dare not to limit yourself to only knowing or doing one thing. Take a chance by putting all you know to use. Accept all invitations to do a new thing and when you do it, celebrate. Move toward your wildest dream, take the labels off your mind and step boldly into your greatness.

With every new step I create a new me.

4 March

One's work may be finished someday but one's
education, never.
– Alexandre Dumas, the Elder

●

Unless you make every waking a learning process, you
are wasting a major portion of your life. You can learn
from people you do not like as well as from those you
love. You can learn from the elders and the youth. You
can learn more about the things you know about and
fine-tune the things you are good at. You can learn by
observing, listening and serving. You can learn by assisting,
completing and forgiving. Never withdraw from the education process by picking and choosing from who you can
learn. Keep your mind open, your ears attuned and your
willingness to learn in the humble state of a student.

I Am learning a little more every day.

5 March

The determination to outwit one's situation means that
one has no models, only object lessons.
– James Baldwin

●

If you are facing a challenge in your life, before asking
someone else what to do, remember what you did the
last time. Nothing is new in life. Everything has been said
or done by you. It may look different. There may be new
people involved. It may even feel different, but it's not.
The key is to recognize the lesson. Ask yourself, 'What
am I learning in this situation?' Is it patience? Peace?
Forgiveness? Independence? What am I feeling now? Have
I felt it before? What did I do then? Remember, no one
can learn your lessons but you. And the best teacher you
will ever have is experience.

*I Am divinely guided at all times and I know exactly
what to do.*

6 *March*

Education is your passport to the future, for tomorrow belongs to the people who prepare for it today.
– El-Hajj Malik El-Shabazz (Malcolm X)

●

Education is not limited to the classroom. It takes place in the kitchen, on the corner, as you ride or walk to any destination, when you listen or speak to others and in the silence of your bedroom. Education springs forth from books, songs, children, elders, women, men. It rises from victory, tragedy, joy and suffering. Education does not take place when you learn something you did not know before. Education is your ability to use what you have learned to be better today than you were yesterday. No matter how much you know or how you learn it, the ultimate goal of education is to give 'you' greater insight to 'yourself.'

I Am educating the world about me.

7 March

You must live within your sacred truth.
– Hausa proverb

●

So much of our time, energy and attention is wasted trying to convince other people how wrong they are about us. We want them to know we are not ignorant, lazy heathens. We want them to retract the untruth that has been told. We try to convince them that we have a valid history, a rich culture and that our ancestors have made valuable contributions to the development of the world. We spend so much time trying to show them who we are not, we lose sight of who we really are. It is not our responsibility to prove to people who we are. Our job and responsibility is to 'be'. What you do is proof of who you are; manifestation is realization. People have a right to think whatever they choose to think. Just because they think it does not make it right.

I Am who I Am.

8 *March*

Sometimes the strong die, too!
– Louis Gossett, Jr

●

Are you one of those people who is always there when somebody needs you? You know just what to say, exactly what to do to turn the worst situation into a conquerable challenge. Everybody calls on you. Everybody needs you. You are, after all, strong enough, smart enough, tough enough to make it through anything and everything. Well, who do the strong go to? Who do the strong lean on? Where do the strong go when they are not feeling very strong? When you set yourself up to be an anchor for everybody else, you jump ship on yourself! The need to be needed, the illusion that without us things would not get done, is actually the way we escape ourselves. The strong have needs. The strong have weaknesses! Sometimes those needs are so deep and painful that, rather than face them, the strong run away. When the strong take the weight of the world on their shoulders, they eventually break down. The question is, Who will be there for the strong?

I take time for me, to do for me the same things I do for others.

9 March

If we stand tall it is because we stand on the backs of
those who came before us.
– Yoruba proverb

●

As painful as it may be to accept, our ancestors were
required to die as part of the evolution of the race. They
died in order that our genius could be spread throughout
the world. They died so that their energy would be shifted
into the invisible, untouchable force that sustains life today.
They died in order that we could stand in a new place,
do new things and create a new order. We must stand
tall knowing the power, strength and wisdom of the ancestors is as close as a breath. All that we ever need to be,
to do, to know, to have is available. All we need do is
take a stand.

I Am standing on a solid foundation.

10 March

Instead of wallowing in my misery, I just made
some changes.
– Stephanie Mills

●

You can do something the same way for so long that
you begin to do it without thinking. When you are not
thinking about what you are doing, you may not recognize its harmful effects. Very often, the habit of doing a
certain thing in a certain way robs you of new experiences. In order to learn to grow and be happy, you must
always seek the new. Take a new route to work today.
Eat lunch in a new environment. Speak to someone before
they speak to you, or let them speak first. Try the radio
instead of television. Bathe in the morning instead of at
night. Be conscious of what you do, how you do it and
be open to happy new experiences.

Today I Am willing to do it differently.

11 March

There are three kinds of people in the world: those who make things happen, those who watch things happen, those who wonder what happened.
– Unknown

●

I was thinking about it but . . . I was going to but . . . I want to but . . . I wish I could but . . . These are the excuses we give for sitting on our butts. We tell ourselves we are waiting for something to happen. We tell ourselves something is missing. We tell other people we will do it, whatever it may be, but we never do. If you think what you need is not there, find it. If you cannot find it, make it. If you cannot make it, find someone who can. If you do not have the money to pay them to make it, get it done on credit. If you have no one to borrow from, ask someone else to borrow it for you. If you do not have credit, get some. If you cannot get credit, go out and do something that someone will pay you for so you can pay for what you need. There are no 'buts' so big they cannot be moved. Once you move the 'butt', everything else will follow.

I would sit here, but I have something to do.

12 *March*

The spirit indeed is willing, but the flesh is weak.
– Matthew 26:41

●

There are many times in life when we want to do,
know we should do, may even know what or how to do,
but we don't. At these times we are relying on the body.
We must realize that the body cannot move without the
spirit. Spirit is the force behind all motion. No matter
what situations we face in this world, spirit is always
with us. That presence is always guiding, protecting, loving
us – to ensure that we do the best. The love of spirit will
inspire us and never abandon our needs. Spirit brings
divine knowing and order so that we can express strength,
peace and power in every situation. When we are fearful
or feeling alone, we can turn within and affirm the love
of spirit. We need never to rely on the physical body
alone, for we are always in the mighty presence of spirit.
Closer than breath, nearer than arms and feet, spirit will
move the body when we ask and obey.

*The guiding love of the spirit within
conquers all without.*

13 March

A man who stands for nothing will fall for anything.
– El-Hajj Malik El-Shabazz (Malcolm X)

●

If you had to tell someone in ten words or less what you stand for in life, what would you say? It might be noble to speak of the liberation for all people of colour, but what do you stand for? Perhaps you would take up the cause of starving or abused children, but what do you stand for? The freedom of political prisoners? Decent housing? Equitable distribution of food and natural resources? An end to all wars and warlike aggression? Or perhaps it's education? It is good, honourable and very noble to have a cause, but before you can do that, you must be able to stand on your own two feet. More battles are lost in this life to weary soldiers than are lost for lack of cause. What do you stand for? How about peace of mind, radiant health, truth and honesty, viable use of your God-given talents, gifts and abilities, or maybe just plain old love. When you are standing on well-cared-for and rested feet, you will be victorious in any cause.

I stand on the principle of me first.

14 March

God is as dependent on you as you are on Him.
– Mahalia Jackson

●

One good way to know whether something is working is to actually see it work. No matter what your philosophy, regardless how much you believe it, if it does not produce, it is worthless. God is the same way. We can talk about Him, sing about Him, pray to Him, for Him and about Him, but if His glory is not produced in our lives, what are we really saying? The only way for God to be seen is through our lives. Our lives must reflect all the things we say God is. We are His hands, feet, eyes and voice. Our lives reflect who and what God is. Are we living a happy life? Are we thinking peaceful thoughts? The only way for God to demonstrate who He is, is for us to do it for Him. We must demonstrate what we know about God in the way we think, talk, walk and live. God is peace. God is strength. God is mercy. God is forgiving. God is all knowing, all powerful, abundant, radiant life. God is love. To know God is to be like Him. All else is a figment of your imagination.

If I want to know who God is, I look at me.

15 March

Truth is more than a mental exercise.
– Thurgood Marshall

●

The human mind is always searching for truth. The mind guides us through books. It interprets our experiences. It limits us based on our exposure. The mind searches to find truth, not realizing that truth was never lost. Unfortunately, truth cannot reveal itself in a mind that is busy with personal chatter. That chatter refers to what you think we need or want and what you say. Unlike truth, your mental chatter may have nothing to do with what is real. The only way to find truth is to go deep within the self and to live from that consciousness and understanding. The truth is the reality of who you are from the inside out, and that is something we rarely think about. Truth is the joy of living, of being, of having a connection to everyone and everything, without thought or malice or condemnation of any part of you. Truth is the spirit of life.

I live in the light of truth.

16 March

If your spiritual philosophy is not moving you to the
state of peace, health, wealth and love your spirit
desires ... you need a new spiritual philosophy.
– Sun Bear

●

What is your spiritual philosophy? Your life philosophy? Is it leading you to the places you want to go? Is it moving you through the challenges and obstacles you face? Is your spiritual philosophy yours? Or is it one that was passed on to you? Is your philosophy creating the optimum conditions in your life? Your spiritual philosophy is the way you approach life. It is the foundation upon which you can stand at any time, in any situation, without fear of falling or failing. If your spiritual philosophy leaves any room for fear, lack, hate, intolerance, anger, pain or shame, it may be time for a change.

I Am open and willing to change.

17 March

Although the face of God is before all people, the fool cannot find it.
– *The Husia*, translated by Dr Maulana Karenga

●

The Creator asks very little of you. He asks that you seek the truth and speak it when you find it. He asks that you treat your brother as you would be treated, forgiving what you need to be forgiven of. He asks that you honour your parents, discipline and value your children, trust and honour yourself as an expression of Him. When you look to anyone or anything as your road to God, you are on your way to being lost. 'Seek ye first the kingdom and all things shall be added.' The kingdom is your heart, free of hate, greed and lust. To find it, you must surrender your wilfulness and listen to the quiet voice within.

I Am One with God.

1 8 March

Spiritual growth results from absorbing and digesting
truth and putting it to practice in daily life.
– White Eagle

●

When there is trouble or trauma, we have a tendency
to become real spiritual. We pray, we say we believe and
usually we collect the miracle we expect. Then we go back
to being our normal human self, doing the same human
things that got us into trouble in the first place. What we
don't understand is that our issues in life are determined
by our consciousness about life. It is only in our moments
of despair that we surrender our humanness. We go to
that higher force, higher consciousness that is within us
all the time. It is quite possible for us to live from that
higher place at all times. We would save ourselves a great
deal of grief if we lived from the truth that we, as humans,
can't do it. Yet through our higher consciousness we are
the conduit. The higher consciousness moves us through
racism, sexism, disease, poverty, fear and confusion. So
why not make that a permanent residence.

I live, move and have by being in a higher authority.

TRUTH

●

Are you living your truth? Is it based on your belief, in the deepest part of your heart? It is that thing you want to be, to do and have about which you rarely speak to anyone. It is that sacred place in your spirit that lets you know no matter what that you are really okay. Are you living your truth? Are you doing what brings you peace and joy? Are you smiling to yourself in the face of adversity, believing you are a divine creation of a loving Father and Mother? Are you beautiful and strong? Powerful and humble? Understanding and merciful? Intelligent and faithful? Protected and prayerful? Is your truth plainly clear and simplistic? Does it bring you the understanding that all is well without when all is well within? Are you living your truth all day, every day, when others tell you it is impossible, impractical, irrelevant and dumb? Is the truth of your being an expression of God? If not, are you really living?

Today I surrender to my truth and live in its being.

20 March

Strategy is better than strength.
– Hausa proverb

●

On the busiest road leading to the village an old wise man sat watching a young man struggling to move logs. The young man sweated, panted and moaned. He called out to the old man, 'Hey, aren't you going to help me get this work done?' The old man smiled and said 'Yes' and continued to sit. A man passed by and greeted the old man with a smile. The old man asked, 'As a favour to an old man, would you move a log?' The man complied, as did the second, the third and so on until all the logs were cleared from the old man's field. The young man saw this and rebuked the old man for being lazy. The wise man smiled and replied, 'If you are in the right place, at the right time, using your assets, the work will get done.'

I Am open to receive all help that comes to me.

21 March

I cry out with my whole heart.
– Psalm 119:145

●

Water purifies. Water nurtures. Water is the healing force of the universe. Water cleanses. Water corrodes. Water refreshes. It is the conduit of growth, protection and maintenance. Crying produces salt water. It purges, protects and expands the spirit. Crying is a release, a cleansing, an expression. However, we must learn to cry with an agenda. Are you crying to release, to purify, to cleanse? Are you angry, frightened, worried or elated? We may cry because of a particular situation, but there is underlying emotion we really need to express. When done properly crying brings clarity and healing to the body and spirit. It can be a refreshing experience, so do it as often as you like. The moment the tears start to flow, just write down your agenda.

When I cry with an agenda, my needs are met.

22 March

God makes three requests of his children: Do the best you can, where you are, with what you have, now.
– African-American folklore

●

There are no guarantees in life, but it is a sure thing that you will get back what you give. If you give 100 percent of your attention, energy and time to a thing, you will get exactly that back. Spending your time and attention focused on what you cannot do and do not have assures that more of the same will come. When you concentrate on lack, weakness, fault and blame, it is sure to become a reality. Nobody has everything, but everybody has something. Use what you have right now! Use it wisely, freely, with love. Wherever you are, use your time, energy and talents to do the best you can right now. Give no thought to what is missing. Spend no time wishing it were better. Make *sure* you give all that you have to make sure you will get all that you need.

I am giving my all right now.

23 March

When you stand with the blessings of your mother and God, it matters not who stands against you.
— Yoruba proverb

●

It is the African way to ask for the blessings of God in everything you do. No child of African descent would attempt an undertaking without the blessings of his or her mother. God and your mother work hand in hand. They created you. They nurtured you. They are your first and eternal teachers. Once God blesses you with the idea and gives you the strength to carry it through, your mother cannot help but want the best for you. If you cannot ask your mother face-to-face, cry out for the blessings of her spirit. When even that is not possible, stand firm and draw your strength from the Mother Earth who will support your good steps without question.

I Am blessed with the strength of God and my mother.

It ain't that I don't believe in God, I just don't
trust his judgment.
– Terry McMillan, from *Mama*

●

There are fifty-one ways to get help from God: (1) Ask
for it; (2) Believe; (3) Recognize help when it comes; (4)
Listen; (5) Obey; (6) Love; (7) Praise; (8) Forgive; (9) Be
Real; (10) Seek Truth; (11) Face yourself; (12) Be Honest;
(13) Order; (14) Understanding; (15) Silence; (16)
Simplicity; (17) Purify; (18) Know; (19) Grace; (20) Joy;
(21) Peace; (22) Trust; (23) Natural Law; (24) Balance;
(25) Harmony; (26) Self-Sufficiency; (27) Dream; (28) Self-
Discovery; (29) Right Thinking; (30) Right Action; (31)
Right Reaction; (32) Breathe; (33) Shut Up; (34) Be Still;
(35) Feel; (36) Live Now; (37) Friends; (38) Parents; (39)
Children; (40) Openness; (41) Realization; (42) Relaxation;
(43) Laugh; (44) Patience; (45) Give; (46) Cry; (47) Create;
(48) Judge Not; (49) Oneness; (50) Faith; (51) Surrender.
Living in and with the ways of God places you in align-
ment with the substance of God.

Help is on the way!

25 March

It is always there.

●

Whenever we need an answer it is there. No matter what the situation, our higher self knows exactly what is best for us. It is not a political, social or intellectual self; it is the core of our being. No matter how long it's been since we consciously communicated with it, the power within us remains steady. Two o'clock on a Saturday morning, it's there. Winter, summer, spring or fall, we've got the power. At the break of day or nightfall, we are guided and protected. There is within a source of light that does not keep a schedule, nine to five, Monday to Friday. It works overtime all the time. It doesn't matter whether we went to church last Sunday or if we haven't been since whenever, if ever. The spirit within is there for us, always. We just have to acknowledge it, praise it, thank it and know everything is all right now.

The spirit is the one and only active power in my life.

26 March

God is always capable of making something
out of nothing.
— Minister Louis Farrakhan

●

'The earth was without form, and void . . .' (Genesis
1:2); today it is a multinational conglomerate. Remember
when there was a void in your life, seemed to be no way
up or out, and then suddenly a way was cleared. What
about when you were down to your last dime and didn't
know where the next one was coming from; it came from
somewhere. When you were at your wits end, the wolves
were on your heels and you had reached the end of your
rope, somehow you rose above it and lived to talk, even
to laugh about it. You may think you did it on your own,
by yourself, without help from anyone, but you didn't
realize where the help was coming from. So the next time
you find yourself in need, ask, who can make something
out of nothing?

I know who can fulfil my needs.

27 March

If you always do what you always did, you will always get what you always got.
– Jackie 'Moms' Mabley

●

Can you imagine not doing what you're doing in your life right now, but doing something completely different? Something exciting, fun, even risky, like quitting your job and travelling around the world. Or working part-time and going to college full time to study scuba diving or basket weaving. Or owning your own home, business, plane or boat. If you can imagine it, why aren't you doing it? I'll tell you why. Because the moment you think about it, you think about all the reasons you can't. 'How will I pay my bills?' 'Who will take care of my family?' 'Where will I get money?' 'What will people say?' Well, here's another question for you, How do you ever expect to be happy or at peace if you stay where you are? If you don't allow yourself to dream, to dare, to move up, out, forward; how will you ever know what you are really capable of? Look at it this way, what's the worse that can happen? You could end up right where you started, doing exactly what you are doing.

Oh, what the heck, go for it anyway.

28 March

Progress means ease, relief, peace, less strife, less struggle and happiness.
– Sufi Hazrat Inayat Khan

●

How many times have you heard someone say, 'That's just the way I am,' or 'I can't change.' How about, 'This is me, take it or leave it!' Oh, how we fight to hold on to what limits us. Don't we realize, if our way worked, it would be working. Can't we see that holding on to what 'I am' keeps us from realizing who we are? It is natural to resist change. It is insane to fight against it. For some reason we believe if we have to change, there must be something wrong with the way we are. The issue is not right or wrong. The issue is working or not working. Everything must change. The best can always be better. The fast becomes fastest. The great becomes the greatest. When we make minor adjustments as we see they are needed, we save time and the expense of a major overhaul.

Behold, I do a new thing.

29 March

Where the mind goes, the behind follows.
– Randolph Wilkerson

●

Whatever situation you find your behind in today, your mind put it there. Your thoughts direct the flow of activity into and out of your life. Your mind can make you ill. Your mind will make you well. Your mind can strengthen your relationships. Your mind will chase all friends and suitors away. Your mind makes you wealthy. Your mind will keep you broke. Your scattered thoughts will create confusion. Dark thoughts will cast out creative light. Thoughts of fear bring negative experiences. Thoughts of enemies bring them to your door. At all times, in all situations, if you don't like where you find your bottom, change what's going on at the top.

I plant positive seeds in the fertile soil of my mind.

30 March

After we fry the fat, we see what is left.
– Yoruba proverb

●

Reading it, saying it, preaching or teaching it does not make it work. The only way to do it is to:

1. Begin within, take quiet time alone.
2. Trust your head, follow your first thought.
3. Don't be fooled by appearances.
4. Plan prayerfully; prepare purposefully; proceed positively; pursue persistently.
5. Be willing to be wrong.
6. Be flexible.
7. Do the best you can where you are with what you have.
8. Be prepared.
9. See the invisible; feel the intangible; achieve the impossible.
10. Focus + Courage + Willingness to Work = Miracles
11. Help somebody else.
12. When in doubt, *pray*.

I've got it now.

31 March

You cannot fix what you will not face.
– James Baldwin

●

The time has come for people of colour to admit the role they play in their own condition. We have been disobedient to the laws of nature, the traditions of the ancestors and the will of God. We have allowed ourselves to remain in situations we know are unproductive out of fear, which is a result of our disobedience, violations of tradition and arrogance in the face of the laws of God. We blamed others for the things we do not do for ourselves. We have betrayed one another to acquire personal riches. We have behaved irresponsibly toward ourselves, have been unaccountable for ourselves, disrespectful toward ourselves by being disobedient and abandoning the word of God. What is God's will? Put the Creator first in all that we do. What is God's law? Do unto others as we would have them do unto us. What is God's word? Love thy brother, and thy sister as you would love yourself. If we are to regain our stature in the world as a proud and mighty people, we must be obedient in following the traditions of the ancestors and we must adhere to the will, laws and word of God.

Today I Am obedient to the ways of God.

1 *April*

As long as you can find someone else to blame for
anything you are doing, you cannot be held
accountable or responsible for your growth or
the lack of it.
– Sun Bear

People of colour must stop blaming everyone else for
their current condition in the world. We cannot forget
our history. We cannot forget the past. We know there
are forces that oppose us, but because they oppose us
does not mean they have won. We must stop believing
what has been said to and about us; we must take full
responsibility for how and what we are. Many people of
colour are afraid to look at the lessons we must learn
from the past. If we do not learn the lessons, we will
continue to repeat the class. We have a reason to be
angry; we have a reason to be afraid; but there is absolutely
no reason for us to remain where we are. When we want
to rise, we will. When we are ready to grow, we can. The
only thing holding us in place right now are the things
'we' do not do.

*If I continue to blame them for where I've been, I can
only blame me for where I go.*

2 April

We have to move beyond the mind-set of powerlessness.
– Audrey Edwards

Have you ever stopped to wonder why children do not concern themselves with all the problems in the world? They seem totally willing to believe that somehow, some way, everything will be fine, and somehow for them it is. Children do not have philosophical ideals, political positions or principles to uphold. They know what they know, they accept it and they never try to convince you that what they know is real. Children ask for what they want; they refuse to take no for an answer; and they know that if you say no, Grandma usually says yes. Children will try anything once. They will go anywhere that looks safe. They are not hung up on styles or profiles, positions and postures, power or powerlessness Yet we believe children don't know, can't do, shouldn't have, can't be, won't make it without us. Isn't it a shame that we don't remember as adults that we are always children of God.

Today I Am a child again.

3 April

Quickened together with him, having forgiven you
all trespasses.
— Colossians 2:13

Black men must forgive Black women for doing what
is necessary for the survival of the race. While it may
appear that the women have been insensitive to and influ-
enced away from the men, it has really been a matter of
doing what was required at any given time. It is the
nature of women to nurture and support. If that support
looks like working in the big houses of the world, learning
how to read and going to school, leaving the men to save
the children, it was necessary at the time. Black men have
an ancestral memory of anger, resentment, guilt, shame
and fear directed toward their grandmothers, mothers
and sisters. How can they feel good about their lovers
and wives? They must forgive. Black men must forgive
Black women for the things they have said and done, for
the things they did not say and do. Black men cannot
accept Black women with the memory of a wounded ego.
They must first forgive. Black men must forgive not for
the sake of the women, but to heal their souls.

Today I see all women through forgiving eyes.

4 *April*

Black women must forgive Black men for not being
there to protect them.
– Suliman Latif

Etched into the memory of our being are the very painful
memories of the past. What they feel like today are:
'Black men are irresponsible.' 'Black men can't be trusted.'
'Black men are no good.' Are we really talking about
Black men today? Or are we remembering those of the
past who were powerless to save our grandmothers from
the events that have created the painful memories? Whether
the memories are from yesteryear, last week or last night,
Black women must individually and collectively forgive
Black men. We must forgive our grandfathers and brothers,
our husbands and sons. If we have anger for one Black
man, we have anger toward them all. We must forgive
Black men for leaving us; we must forgive them for the
excuses they did not make. We must forgive Black men
for the things they say; we must forgive them for the
things they do not do. Forgiveness is the only way to free
ourselves and our masculine complements from the atroc-
ities committed against our mutual souls.

There is a place of forgiveness within me. Today I
lovingly share it with Black men.

5 April

You will never know who you are in the world until you know thyself.
– Dr John Henry Clarke

We are descendants of the parent race, Africans, transported to a new land. We are African-Americans, African-Caribbeans, African-Latinos and Africans natively. Over the course of the last thirty years we have become eager to embrace our ancestral roots. That is good. It is not good, however, that we continue to define our 'Africanness' in concepts foreign to us. We claim the music, dance, art and clothing. Yet we become uncomfortable about discussing the so-called dark side of the motherland—rituals, scarification, wearing leaves and animal skins, root medicine, bones in the nose, animal sacrifice, plates in the lips and tribalism. We shy away from what we have come to understand is still unacceptable by other standards. We must study ourselves, for ourselves. Until that time, it will remain difficult, confusing and uncomfortable to accept or reject the place we call 'Mother'.

From my darkness comes the light.

6 *April*

Intuition is the spiritual faculty that does not explain,
it simply points the way.
– Florence Scoval Schinn

Nia had been prepared to inherit the wise woman's book. The old woman was the salvation and the backbone of the entire village. She was wise. She was loved. But she had become too old to carry out her duties. In return for twenty-two years of training, Nia was to inherit the old woman's key to life. The ceremony was long. The people were many. The responsibility was great. Nia was prepared. She was eager to get started. She believed the book would reveal the answers to all of life's questions. It required two strong men to carry the book to her chamber. When they placed it on her table, she quickly waved them away. The book was solid gold, trimmed with emeralds, rubies and sapphires. In the middle of the front cover sat a seven-carat diamond. Nia's heart was pounding. Her mouth had gone dry. With her eyes closed, she fondled the cover of the book. The time had come to open it. She was about to learn life's secret. She opened to the middle of the book. She looked down at the page. Nia had inherited a book of mirrors.

The storehouse of abundance is already mine.

7 April

Our greatest problems in life come not so much from
the situations we confront as from our doubts about
our ability to handle them.
– Susan Taylor

It makes perfectly good sense to get directions when
you are travelling to a new place. Culture and heritage
are directions that will help you move forward. You have
a rich culture and a powerful heritage. Yet we forget that
our ancestors built the world, healed the sick and educated
the ignorant. Why should we forget the African minds,
bodies and spirits of the past who paved the way into
today? We must accept and understand that they didn't
do it 'because' they were Africans; rather, they were
Africans and they knew how. Culture is a rock in a hard
place, and we know the Africans knew a great deal about
rocks. Let us stand on the knowing of our ancestors,
remembering the heritage of the people, the traditions of
the family, and the wisdom and strength they used to
make it through the rough days.

I know what the ancestors would do.

Every time I had the good fortune to research into someone's religion I found 'God' to be in the image of the people to whom the religion belongs.
– Yosef Ben-Jochannon

Would the Creator, with all the love, power and wisdom of the universe, make us all so different and then deem only one right way to get to His kingdom? I would think not. As an expression of the awesome power of the ultimate creative energy, we the people have been blessed to bring forth various expressions. We call it race, culture, tradition and heritage. In essence, who we are collectively is a unique expression of God. No one knows better than He the beauty we bring to life, and He cannot be wrong. As we lift our minds and hearts to know, to be aware and to understand that we are all expressions of the Most High, we will begin to recognize the beauty of God at our disposal. Our world reflects God's strength as tradition, God's wisdom as culture, God's love as race and ethnicity. Who are we to decide which part of God is the best?

God's strength, wisdom, power and love are being expressed as me.

9 April

A strong man masters others. A truly wise man
masters himself.
– *The Wisdom of the Taoists*

There are so many scars inside of people of colour, it
is incredible that we survive. Scars from childhood memories. Scars from dreams deferred. Scars from words, inci-
dents and our judgments of them. We cover the scars
with personality, habits, and sometimes, drugs, sex and
alcohol. We take our wounded souls into the world and
pretend that we are not hurt. Yet every time we are
confronted with an event similar to the one that caused
the scars, the wounds are reopened. There can be no
healing in our external world until we give intensive care
and healing to our internal wounds. We may think we
do not know what to do. We do. We must first admit
that the wounds exist. We must be willing to examine
them, touch them and expose them to ourselves. Then
we must wrap them in the most potent antiseptic there
is – love.

Today I will nurture my wounds with love's light.

10 April

Until you free yourself from the final monster in the jungle of your life, your soul is up for grabs.
– Rona Barrett

Many of us do not realize we have a problem because the way we live is a reflection of what we have lived with. There are men who don't know they are abusive. There are women who do not know they are being abused. There are people who don't know how to take care of themselves. There are people who believe just getting by is fine. There are children who think it is okay that they are not nurtured. There are people who do not know how to ask for what they need. There are people who fall down and never try to get up. There are people who get up by stepping on the people who fell down. Each one of us believes we are fine just the way we are, so we make no effort to get better. If the world and how it works is a reflection of the people who live in it, what will it take for us to realize we have a lot of work to do?

Today I will take a long, hard look at me.

11 April

We are the children of those who chose to survive.
– Nana Poussaint in *Daughters of the Dust*

If you have ever doubted your ability to survive, look at who you came from. Don't limit yourself to parents and grandparents, go all the way back to the root. In your family line is the genius of those who were born into a barren land and built the Pyramids. In the oasis of your mind is the consciousness of those who charted the stars, kept time by the sun and planted by the moon. In the centre of your being is the strength of those who planted the crops, toiled in the fields and banqueted on what others discarded. In the light of your heart is the love of those who bore the children who were sold away only to one day hang from a tree. In the cells of your bloodstream is the memory of those who weathered the voyage, stood on the blocks, found their way through the forest and took their case to the Supreme Court. With all of that going for you, what are you worrying about?

I move in the power of a mighty past.

12 April

Rather than face how bad I truly felt about me, I stuffed myself with stuff, puffed myself up with a false sense of power and importance.
– Patti Austin

Many people of colour believe they are lacking something. We have been programmed to feel that way. We are taught we lack good looks. We are led to believe we lack intelligence. We are educated in a system that denies our history, culture and traditions. How are we expected to feel complete? We are not! We are, however, expected to look good on the outside. We do. We dress up to hide our inner feelings of inadequacy. We are led to believe that if we have a home, a car, a few jewels and nice clothes we have enough to matter. It doesn't work! In order for people of colour to thrive rather than survive, to flourish rather than make it, to stand tall rather than just stand up, we must individually and collectively get rid of the stuff and get to the core – what does it really feel like to be a person of colour?

I Am in touch with my feelings about who I am.

13 April

We are living in a world where your colour matters
more than your character.
– Sister Souljah

People want you to believe that colour doesn't matter.
It shouldn't, but it does. We cannot get away from the
colour question. The question is, who does it matter to?
Does it matter to you that you come from a rich tradition of proud people who believe in self-determination?
Does it matter to you that your ancestral culture is based
on a spirit of support and respect? Does it matter to you
that you are genetically coded for genius, thereby rendering
you capable of realizing physical, intellectual and spiritual perfection? Does it matter to you that you are the
keeper of a legacy of worldwide accomplishments? Does
it matter to you that you have the God-given right, by
virtue of your colour, to glorify, magnify and fortify the
legacy that you have inherited as a descendant of the first
doctors, chemists, agriculturists, astronomers, astrologers,
artisans, teachers and spiritual masters? Or does it matter
only to those who tell you what you cannot do because
of your colour?

I really do matter.

14 April

You must act as if it is impossible to fail.
— Ashanti proverb

The truth is that we start from a position of success. No matter what happens, no matter what the appearance, we are always successful. The truth is that we have lessons to learn through our experiences. What appears as a failure is simply a stepping stone to realizing success. The truth is that we can do anything we focus our mind to do. What looks like failure teaches us what not to do, what does not work. It sends us back to the drawing board. It forces us to refocus, and redo. All circumstances in the physical world are subject to change. The truth, however, is consistent. It never changes. The truth is that, as long as we are breathing, we are one with God. God never fails. Our job is to act like we know.

Victory is the stuff I am made of.

15 April

In a moment of decision, the best thing you can do
is the right thing to do. The worst thing you can do
is nothing.
– Theodore Roosevelt

We always want to do the right thing, but we do the
wrong thing when we do not make a decision about what
to do. Decisions have power. Decisions have force. They
usually take us to the exact place we need to be, exactly
the way we need to get there. It is the wavering back and
forth that is dangerous. It places us at the mercy of events;
we fall prey to the choices people make for us. Since time
and opportunity wait for no one, our lives will not stand
still until we figure out what to do. The rightness of a
decision is based on our ability to make the decision.
When we weigh what we want against what we will have
to do, a decision can be an effortless event. We must
know what we will and will not do, what we can do and
choose not to do; and decide in harmony with the things
we know. The freedom from making a decision can only
come after we have made the decision.

Today I decide to be free from all decisions.

16 April

Your world is as big as you make it.
– Georgia Douglas Johnson

Guess what? You are not the worst person in the world! Sure, you've made some bad judgment calls, taken some pretty foolish chances, created some awful situations, but you give yourself too much credit. Others have done far worse. Then there are those people who haven't done anything to anybody – ever. They are quiet. Go unnoticed. They have flawless characters and records. But you know what? They haven't done anything for themselves either. They are probably just as, if not more, miserable and confused as you. Think about it this way: The future will be what you make it today. Whether you are a doer or a non-doer, you must work on your future. If you've made a mess, clean it up. If you are afraid to take a chance, take one anyway. If you've done things that didn't work, do something else. If you have done nothing, do something. What you don't do can create the same regrets as the mistakes you make. In the long run, either you must happen to life, or it will never happen for you.

Step by step, I Am getting better and better.

When the shoe fits, we forget about the feet.
— *The Wisdom of the Taoists*

Many of us look at life as work. We approach it and try to handle it like a job. We complain about it. We blame others when it is not working. We hold someone else responsible when it does not give us what we want. Some of us give up on life. We move from day to day, with no plan, no goals and ultimately no rewards. We fail to understand that if life is work, the better we do it, the better it will pay us. When we perform our tasks to the very best of our ability we receive just rewards for what we do. When we are thorough in our work and put our best into it, we become better at it. When we become too good for where we are, we will be advanced to our rightful place. The things we must realize about life is it cannot be better until we are better. We cannot get more until we are more. The only thing that can stop our advancement in life is our not being ready to move. If life is work, run it like a multimillion-dollar corporation and elect yourself chief executive officer.

The better I Am at life the better it gets.

18 April

Life has to be lived, that's all there is to it.
– Eleanor Roosevelt

Let's be honest, we don't really want to work at life.
Work is hard. Work is tiring. We want to have fun. We
want to play! We want to have a good time and have all
the things we want. Why not play the game of life? We
are the dealers. We hold all the cards. Somewhere along
the line, somebody cheated us. They told us we were
needy, helpless and dependant. That is baggage. We must
put it down in order to deal ourselves a good hand. We
must also know the rules. We must play fairly, dealing
with everyone the way we want to be dealt with. We
must expect to win. If we entertain failure at any point,
we lose. When we play, we must be on the lookout for
fouls. When we see a foul, we must call it. We don't have
to fix it, but we must call it. The final and most important rule is that we must follow all the rules, all the time.

When I play by the rules, I win.

19 April

In the province of the mind, what one believes to be
true either is true or becomes true.
– John Lilly

What do you believe about the world? Do you believe
it is big and beautiful? Or that it is dangerously doomed?
Do you believe there are people out there waiting to get
you? What do you think they will do with you when they
get you? Do you believe you can't because they won't let
you? Do you believe you can because nobody can stop
you? Do you believe in choices or in the power of destiny?
Do you believe in evil? Do you believe you are free? Do
you believe that someday, somehow you will be what and
where you want to be? Do you believe that someone else
has more power than you? How much power do you
believe you have? What you believe will come true whether
it is good or not so good. What you believe about the
world is exactly what you will experience because that is
what 'you' bring into the world.

The world as I see it is a reflection of my thoughts.

20 April

The one who asks questions doesn't lose his way.
– Akan proverb

Because we don't want to seem stupid, uninformed or feel belittled, we don't like to ask questions. For some reason, we think we are supposed to know everything. When we don't, we don't let anyone know. Questions are not a sign of ignorance. They are an indication that you are broadening your scope, sharpening your skills, improving your capabilities. Enquiries indicate humility, the willingness to serve, share and support. Questions keep you on track, define and broaden your boundaries and remove limitations. Questions put you in touch and keep you in touch. Questions create and build resources, both natural and human, which can be very useful when there is no one around to answer your questions. Your ego, the nasty little voice that is overconcerned with what other people think, will tell you not to ask questions. Tell ego to shut up and then ask what you need to know.

Who? What? Where? When? How? Why?

21 April

The cost of liberty is less than the price of repression.
– W.E.B. DuBois

Repression of your will and desire are the cornerstones of stress. When you believe or are led to believe you are unable to act upon the greatest desires of the soul, the result is mental and spiritual enslavement. The price you pay for your enslavement is your self-dignity, self-respect and self-esteem. To be free, you must acknowledge your personal liberty as the God-given right it is. You must be willing to take a stand for yourself. When you stand, you must be responsible for yourself. Liberty is the God-given right to declare who you are and to pursue what you want. If you surrender that right, you repress yourself.

I Am the only one who can limit me.

22 April

The bell rings loudest in your own home.
– Yoruba proverb

As you look around the community, society, the world, you probably see many things you would like to change. Injustice, inequality, hatred and poverty probably disturb you. You may be angered by the lack of respect and insensitivity to people and their needs. You want to speak out and sometimes strike out to make the changes happen, but don't forget that God works from the inside out. You must first look within yourself to eliminate the fear, the anger, the imbalance in your life. Then and only then can you move forward to create peacefully and powerfully the changes needed in the world.

The world I want begins within me.

23 April

It is far better to be free to govern or misgovern yourself than to be governed by anybody else.
– Kwame Nkrumah

When you look at the world, it is very easy to see what
is not being done for you. When your needs are not met,
when your interests are not being served, there is a tendency
to complain. If the one entrusted to serve, protect and
guide you promotes his own interests above yours, you
learn to do for yourself. It matters not what experience
you lack. Your interests will guide you. Give no concern
to what they say you cannot do. Be willing to accept the
challenge. Do not be afraid to question the process. New
systems are born from the questioning of the old. Take
time to retreat to that quiet place within the pit of your
soul and unleash your right to decide what is best for you.

I Am the source of my own governance.

24 April

Men build institutions . . . so that four hundred years later their descendants can say, 'That's what he left.'
– Na'im Akbar

Frederick Douglass warned us many years ago that as long as we are not the direct beneficiaries of the fruits of our labour, we will remain slaves. There is something insidious about a contentment with working 'for' someone throughout your life. Silently it says, 'You need me.' It is embedded in your consciousness, 'You can't do without me.' Eventually you believe, 'I'm not capable of taking care of myself.' Eventually you stop trying. The world needs the kind of institutions men of colour can build. Whether it is a business to be managed, a school to be staffed, a publication to be circulated, an organization to be advanced or a service to be carried out, men want more from the world than a gold watch and a fond memory.

I am building more than a nest egg.

25 April

Fewness of words, Greatness of deeds.
– Abdul Baha

What are you waiting for? With all you say you want,
there is:

A dream for you to follow;
A goal for you to set;
A plan for you to make;
A project for you to begin;
An idea for you to act on;
A possibility for you to explore;
An opportunity for you to grab;
A choice for you to make.

If not, you shouldn't have anything to talk about.

*Today I will make it my business to say less
and do more.*

26 April

You must realize what is actually going on before you
can effectively deal with it.
– Ralpha

When our fears, weaknesses and views about life are
coloured by low self-esteem or lack of self-worth, we are
restricted. It seems as though we have a road map that
leads to nowhere. What we don't always realize is that
we have created the road. It is a reflection of what we
think about ourselves. We measure the future by the
errors of the past. We make agreements with ourselves
or others, which we do not keep. We surround ourselves
with people and situations that degrade, devalue and limit
us. Then we question why we have no confidence. No
matter what race we are or what other people think or
say about us, the first limitations we must overcome are
those we place on ourselves.

New patterns of living are open to me.

27 April

I cannot win anything until I am willing to
lose everything.
– Kennedy Schultz

For some reason, we believe struggle is noble. We think
it brings special rewards or that the God force is pleased
with us when we struggle. Struggling people have so
much to do and say about the things they are struggling
with that they hardly have time to get anything done.
Struggling people know how to struggle well. They know
what to wear, where to go and how to behave in a way
that will undoubtedly create more struggle. Struggling
people impose conditions, restrictions and expectations
upon themselves, because it is easier to struggle doing
nothing than it is to bring up and use the creative force
within. Struggling people love to sacrifice in the name of
the struggle. They sacrifice themselves, their families and
if you are not careful, they will sacrifice you. God does
not ask us to struggle. What we are told is, 'Come up to
Me all ye that labour and I will give ye rest.'

I ain't gonna struggle no more.

28 April

You can't solve the problem because you
don't know what it is.
— *A Course in Miracles*

Does it ever seem that as soon as you solve one crisis, another pops up? What about the way you think about the challenges in your life? Do you think it's money, or the lack of it? When you get the money together, the kids or maybe the spouse act up. As soon as they calm down, it's the job or the car or the pipes in the basement. You can spend the better part of your life putting out little brushfires with your kettle without ever realizing there is a forest fire burning in your life. By now you should have realized you cannot solve the problems in your life. No matter how hard you try, you cannot do it. Want to know why? It is because you think you are in control when you really aren't. There is a divine source, a powerful force, a perfect order that controls everything. When you recognize it, acknowledge it and surrender to it, you won't have to struggle to solve problems. There won't be any.

*The universe will perfect that which concerns me when
I surrender control.*

Identification with an organization or a cause is no substitute for self-realization.
– Swami Rudrananda

People of colour have many causes to battle, confront and overcome – or so we think. We keep bringing up causes and creating organizations to address them; however, most of us take very little time to look at ourselves. Throughout history there have been myriad physical and spiritual forces that have drained us. Yet when we feel drained we try to keep busy. We find a cause to work on or a group to join, taking our drained, imbalanced energy along. Self-realization requires that we break down everything we identify with in order to understand where we are and how we feel about being there. We must free ourselves from all encumbrances in order to look within and discover the mental and spiritual freedom that is our birthright. When we are free from cause identification and organizational duty, we will know for sure exactly who we are and where we should be. Self-realization puts us back in touch with our first cause, the self.

Anything I hang on to will get in my way.

30 April

When you are down and out lift up your head and
shout, 'I'm Outta Here!'
– Lynette Harris

I'm outta here! It really is just that simple. There comes
a point in life when you get tired of feeling, doing and
looking bad. When that time comes, you move on instantly.
I'm outta here is an affirmation. A statement of truth. It
gives power to your decision to no longer be where you
are physically, mentally and emotionally. I'm outta here
puts the world on notice that you have a commitment to
be better, do better, have more than you have right now.
Debt – I'm outta here! Make a budget and payment plan.
Stick to it. Illnesses – I'm outta here! Take responsibility,
not pills, for what ails you. Find out what you are doing
that is not good for you and stop. Lousy job – I'm outta
here! Figure out what you like to do, want to do and
what you are good at and do it. Struggle – I'm outta
here. Do not beat up on yourself. Do not criticize yourself. Above all, do not limit yourself. Pick yourself up.
Put yourself on a path and let yourself know –

I'm outta here!

1 May

For unto whomsoever much is given, of him shall
much be required.
– Luke 12:48

Have you ever wondered why certain people are
expected to do things a little faster or better than everyone
else? The simple answer is because they can. Have you
ever wondered why you are expected to do the impossible, achieve the unattainable or overcome the insurmountable? Very simply because you can. You know how
you can just look at somebody and know they can do
it? Well, the exact same thing is true about you.
Unfortunately, we are not always aware of just how
magnificent we are. The same light others see shining
blinds us about ourselves. We become content being like
everyone else when something inside tells us we are not.
But we plod along being angry or bitter when others
expect us to do what they cannot. The key is not to do
what others do and say; it is to know we can, believe we
can and do what we can to the best of our ability. If we
know what to expect from ourselves, we will always live
up to our greatest expectation.

I am expecting as much as I can because I can.

2 May

LENT = Let's Eliminate Negative Thinking.
– Earl Nightingale

When you think negatively, you attract negativity. That is the awesome power of the mind. When you confront the world with negative thoughts, you will have experiences to confirm what you are thinking. Thought to experience, that is the process. It is not the other way around. What you believe people and the world are doing to you is actually a reflection of what your thoughts are drawing to you. If you want to free yourself from the harshness of the world, clear harsh thoughts from your mind. Clear anger with forgiveness, confusion with orderly thinking. Clear restriction with an open mind, violence with peaceful thoughts. Clear denial with acceptance, hate with thoughts of love. When you clear what you do not want from the recesses of your mind, it will miraculously disappear from your life.

I will think negativity out of my way.

3 May

No man can serve two masters ... or else he will hold
to the one, and despise the other.
– Matthew 6:24

You cannot love while hating, progress while oppressing,
come together in disunity, build while tearing down, join
while separating, understand while not listening, give while
withholding, create while destroying, overcome while in
fear. It is simply impossible! People of colour must make
a choice: Either we accept what we believe others are
doing to us, or reject it and do something else. If we love
each other as a foundation for our own progress, we do
not have to worry about others hating us or our hating
them back. If we work with everyone for human good,
giving what we can to create what we want, we will not
be disturbed by what anyone attempts to keep from us.
If we stand on the faith of our ability to survive, it does
not matter who is out to destroy us. If we celebrate,
support and nurture ourselves, we will not need anyone
else to do it for us.

Today I will feel one thing at a time.

4 May

You can be so heavenly bound until you are
no earthly good.
– Dr Oscar Lane

We can find so many reasons to postpone doing and receiving our good:

'It's not the right time.'
'If it's for me, I'll get it.'
'I'm waiting for a sign.'
'I'll do it later.'
'I'll receive my rewards in heaven.'
'I guess it's not for me.'
'I didn't want it/need it anyway.'

These are just a few of the ways we convince ourselves not to follow our dreams. The belief in a hereafter paved with gold is no reason to live in poverty now. 'As above, so below' means whatever we can have later, we can have right now. If heaven is a place prepared for kings and queens, we want to do our work on earth so we won't show up looking and acting like paupers.

There is no earthly reason for me to delay my good.

5 May

When the door is closed, you must learn to slide across
the crack of the sill.
– Yoruba proverb

Human beings are creatures of habit. We do what we
know, what is comfortable and what we 'think' will work.
There are, however, those occasions when 'our' way is
not 'the' way to get us to the goal. When your way
doesn't work, don't be disheartened. You must be willing
to try another way. Don't be discouraged when someone
says 'no'. Be willing to ask someone else. Always be
willing to start at the bottom. Being willing does not
mean you will stay there. A closed door does not mean
you have been cut off permanently. It is a challenge, an
obstacle, a tool to be used. The keys to all doors are
within you. If you have faith in yourself, practice and
patience will make you a master locksmith.

*I Am willing to do it by any means honourable
and necessary.*

Faith without work cannot be called faith.
– *The New Open Bible*

Faith must inspire action. It alone cannot be verbal. Mental faith is insufficient. Faith is not believing, trying or hoping. It is the knowing by which you do. Faith develops endurance to face the trials without being tempted to stop. Faith produces doers. Those who understand fewness of words, greatness of deeds are a measure of true faith. Faith is obedience to the urgings of the spirit, the porthole through which all things have their being. Faith controls the tongue, soothes the head and stifles the lust to complain. Faith produces patience. Your life is the only true measure of your faith. Your words and actions determine the fullness of your cup. If there is anyone or anything of unworthiness in your life you must ask yourself, 'To what am I giving my faith?'

I put my faith in only those things that produce good for me.

TRUST

Have you ever worried whether there would be enough air for you to breathe? How often do you ponder what you would do if the laws of gravity ceased to operate? For some reason, you never worry about the very essential elements you need to stay alive. You just trust they will be there, and they are. You trust that your heart will beat, your blood will flow, your lungs will expand and that you will stay firmly planted on the earth. You trust that every organ within you will do exactly as it should. You trust that your body will support you. Why not extend that trust to every area of your life? Trust that the universe and Creator will provide everything that you need without any effort on your part. All you ever need do is ask and trust.

As I trust, my needs are met.

8 May

You must eat the elephant one bite at a time.
– Twi proverb

   You cannot get to the end from the middle. You won't find the beginning at the end. No matter what we arc doing, there is a process. Whether the situation is positive or negative, we must go through the process. When we rush ahead we miss important steps. If we become impatient, we can overlook details. We must be willing to move step by step, inch by inch to get to the end. There is no way to rush the process. When we are excited, we want to see how a situation will end. When the situation is unpleasant, we want it to end quickly. Whether anxiety or fear, the anticipation of benefits or pain, no matter what we do, we must be willing to do it one step at a time.

An inch is a cinch, a yard is hard.

9 May

That my joy might remain in you, and that
your joy might be full.
– John 15:11

Waiting for a particular turn of events is a good way
to lead yourself into disappointment. Depending on anyone
to make you happy, make you feel good or lift your spirit
is a sure way to place yourself in isolation. When your
joy is dependent on people and conditions, it is restricted.
Joy must spring forth from you before it can surround
you. Joy must be the way you walk and the way you
speak to those who come into your realm. Joy is knowing
you are doing what you can, the best you can, and you
are feeling good about it. Joy is knowing time is on your
side and wherever you are, you are the joy. Joy is taking
a moment to say thank you, a day to do for self and an
energy of sharing what you have. Joy is not what happens
to you; it is what comes through you when you are
conscious of the blessing you are.

I Am the source of joy.

10 May

Grandma's hands used to issue out a warning,
baby don't you run so fast, there might be
snakes in that grass . . .
– Bill Withers

We cannot rush the sunrise or pay to bring on the full moon. Winter knows exactly when to turn into spring and nothing can coax the grass to come up before it's ready. As we move through life, we must accept that everything will happen when it is supposed to happen. Accepting that will teach us patience. Days and nights whiz by. Frenzied minds, pressured people come and go. Worry, anxiety and fear do not concern the laws of nature. Nature knows that destiny takes its time. The key to patience is trusting the inner presence that knows exactly what you need. That inner presence allows everything to unfold divinely at just the right time. Be patient and trust you will get exactly what you want, especially if the 'great' grandmothers have anything to say about it.

I wait patiently on my good.

11 May

Spirit works on a full-time basis.

Life requires that we spend parts of our time doing certain things. We work sometimes, go to school at times; we are children or parents and friends part time. The one area of life that cannot be addressed on a part-time basis is the spiritual life. To be a part-time Christian, Buddhist, Muslim or anything else results in 'a house divided against itself', which cannot stand. The spiritual house is the mind and it requires constant care. Spiritual conviction is the manner in which the house is run. When you have a spiritual conviction, it will serve you in all situations, all day, every day, in every way. The same spirit that guides your family life must also run your social life. If you turn to spirit for financial guidance, you must also ask for professional guidance. If you let spirit pick your friends, you must trust it to pick your mate. Part-time spirituality creates inner turmoil, indecision, confusion and stagnation. Once we let spirit take over full time, we will find life is more enjoyable and peaceful than we ever thought possible.

I let go and let spirit guide me every day in every way.

12 May

Pride that you express to others is ego. Pride that you
express silently to yourself is real pride.
– Stuart Wilde

When you are proud of yourself, you show it, you feel
it and you know it. It shines in your eyes, the way you
speak and the way you carry your very being. You are
proud because you could and you did, you can and you
will, you cannot but you know it, and it is still okay.
When you are proud you do, give and share rather than
take, talk and promise. Pride is peaceful service, joy-filled
sharing, inner knowing that there is more to come. Pride
does not argue to be right, push to get ahead, step over
others to get there and forget them once it does. Pride is
gentle, calm and balanced. It is not boastful, frightened
or hurried. Pride is pleasant. Pride is grateful. Pride is
peaceful, patient and poised. Pride is secure. Pride is
mastery, but most of all, pride is silent.

I am gently, calmly, silently proud of me
and what I Am.

13 May

I am not a special person. I am a regular person
who does special things.
– Sarah Vaughan

Most of us want to be singled out, patted on the back
and rewarded for what we do. It may never happen;
however, that does not mean what we do is not valuable
or worthy of recognition. No one is special in God's eyes.
We are all provided with the ability to do. What we have
not been taught is to do good just for the sake of doing
it, without pursuing rewards or recognition. When you
do what you can for the sake of doing it, the reward is
an improvement of the skills. When you use what you
know to do what you can and someone else benefits, that
is recognition. We all have a need to be appreciated for
the contributions we make to the world. We must learn
to recognize our own value before the world can respond
to our needs. Some of us will plant the seed and never
see the plant. Some of us will harvest the crop without
knowing the planter. Some of us will eat the plant, paying
someone else to prepare it. When the process is complete
we will all be rewarded, recognizing how special the process
has been to all.

I do my part. I Am rewarded when others do theirs.

14 May

The ego needs recognition. The spirit does not need to
thank itself.
– Stuart Wilde

The ego wants to be noticed. It needs stroking, pumping
up and limelight. The ego needs to compete just to prove
it is better. It senses danger around every corner, difficulty in every challenge and trouble coming through
everyone. The ego can never be enough, do enough or
have enough. The goal of the ego is to be well liked and
authorized because, for some reason, it does not feel qualified. The spirit is qualified by light. The light of truth,
peace, joy and love. It does not seek to condemn, condone
or compromise what it is. It simply knows and is it. The
spirit does what it can and moves on to something else.
It does not ask for an award or wait for rewards, it is
just spirit being spirit. One of the difficult problems in
the world is the competition of egos. They want to be
noticed and applauded so they compete and dominate.
When we truly understand that we are spiritual beings,
we will no longer have a need for recognition. We will
do what we can because we can do it by virtue of the
light of spirit.

Today I will go unnoticed.

15 May

With your hands you make your success, with your
hands you destroy success.
—Yoruba proverb

The key to success is not what you do, it is how you
feel about what you are doing. It is possible to take a
simple idea and create a huge success. We think people
who accomplish this work hard or have others to support
them. We believe they are smarter, richer or in some way
more endowed than we are. What we cannot see and do
not measure is people's attitudes about what they do.
Success begins with a positive attitude, it is the most valuable asset we may own. The people at the top did not
fall there. They were· willing to do whatever it took,
taking the ups and the downs, asking for what they really
wanted and staying focused until they got it. Success is
not bought or inherited. It is a product of what we put
out. Success begins with a good feeling about where we
are and a positive attitude about where we want to be.

My success is worth the effort of a positive mind and a
genuine smile.

16 May

When you don't have a grip on life, it will definitely
get a grip on you.
– Jewel Diamond-Taylor

Life is:

A mystery, Unfold it.
A journey, Walk it.
Painful, Endure it.
Beautiful, See it.
A joke, Laugh at it.
A song, Sing it.
A flower, Smell it.
Wonderful, Enjoy it.
A candle, Light it.
Precious, Don't waste it.
A gift, Open it.
Love, Give it.
Unlimited, Go for it.
Light, Shine in it.

I Am all that life is.

17 May

Ain't gonna let nobody turn me around . . .
—African-American spiritual

Some mornings we wake up feeling good, ready to go out and take on the world and 'be' a great day. But on others days we wake up to a greyness that makes the whole world seem depressing. On those dark days we need to remember: 'Every day is a blessing to behold.' We must realize that the attitude with which we greet the day says a great deal about what the day will be like. We make our days pleasant or miserable. If we insist on being miserable, irritable and nasty, more than likely the day will give us exactly what we give it. When we start the day with a spirit of joy, openness, peace and love, we put the universe on alert, we want more of the same. A day is too valuable to waste on misery and unhappiness. Even misery cannot stand up to a happy face and heart.

Today is a great day full of great people and events.

18 May

Examine the labels you apply to yourself. Every label is a boundary or limit you will not let yourself cross.
– Dwayne Dyer

You are first of all a human. That gives you a certain amount of power. You are not limited in how you express your humanness; you are limited by the labels you choose to describe it. Men do this, Women do that . . . Blacks like one thing, Asians like the other . . . Native Americans are proud, Latinos are rowdy. These views and labels limit the self and set up expectations from others. You are never too old or too young, rich or poor, too much of a man or woman to think. You can be anything and everything you think you can be when you don't think yourself into a book. You must keep reminding yourself that you are more than a body. You are more than an image. You are more than the things you have told yourself about yourself. You are a spirit expressing as a human being. And that, my dear, is unlimited.

I Am a no-name brand of human being.

19 May

Help your friends with the things that you know, for
you know these things by Grace.
—*The Maxims of Ptahhotpe*

At a time when unity is so desperately needed it is
significantly lacking. Misunderstandings about basic philosophical differences place people on opposite poles.
Competition for perceived limited resources separate
people along racial, social and gender lines. The need to
be right and feel supported separates us from those who
hold different views and opinions. Our internal obstacles
and external oppositions create a debilitating conflict and
limits the coming together of the people of the world. If
each of us would take the time to examine our feelings,
we would see that 'they' are right, too. The nature, experiences and perceptions of individuals help mould the
ideals they hold. If we could remember and respect this
right for everyone, we could avoid open confrontations.
There are so many causes and issues in the world and so
many ways to approach them, it is unlikely we will all
agree on one way. Unity does not mean we will all believe
in or do the same thing. It means we will agree to do
something without battling over how and why.

All roads lead to the end.

20 May

Natural beauty comes in all colours, strength in many forms. When we learn to honour the differences and appreciate the mix, we're in harmony.
– Unknown

Spiritually, we are all family. We are mother, father, brother, sister and children of one another. As spiritual family we are inseparable. We all breathe the same air that is connected to the same Source; we are all connected to the same Source by the rhythm of breath. Just like a family, we will have our differences, yet we can be different and still be a family. Just like a family, we will have our rebels and outcasts, but we must still include them in the family circle. Just as a family sits and eats together, we must make certain that there is enough for everyone. Just as a family comes together and shares, we must stop holding back and taking away from the family. Blood may be thicker than water, but it is the water of life that will keep us connected. As we learn to see each other through our spiritual eyes, the physical differences will cease to matter.

Today I will honour all of my relations.

21 May

I am the one whose mouth is pure and
hands are clean.
– *The Book of Coming Forth by Day*, translated by
Maulana Karenga

As we pass through the sea of life, we meet many types of fish. Mud fish sling dirt in order to keep themselves clean. Guppies have big mouths that are always moving, but guppies are always being eaten up by bigger fish. Barracudas knock you out of the way, get in the way and never go away. Eels slither around on their bellies, eating what others leave behind. They do nothing for themselves, so they want what you have. Crabs move from side to side. Today they are on your side, the next day they are not. Flounder have both eyes on one side of their heads. They can only see things one way. Crayfish move backwards. Sea horses eat their own. Whales blow air out of the top of their heads. Sharks attack all other fish. Angel fish float around with no idea of what is going on. Then there are the salmon. They always swim upstream; and no matter how far they swim, they never forget how to come home.

I know who I am in the sea of life.

The bumblebee's wings are so thin and its body so big, it should not be able to fly. The only problem is, the bee doesn't know that.
– David Lindsey

Most of us do not know what we cannot do until someone tells us. We are willing to try almost anything, go anywhere, stretch ourselves to the limits in pursuit of our dreams. And then we talk to other people. We are reminded of how dangerous it may be, how ridiculous it sounds, what a chance we are taking. People have no problem informing us of all the downsides and pitfalls; they cannot see how we will ever reach the goal. They put us in touch with our faults, limitations and habits. They remind us of all the others who didn't make it, and in vivid detail they tell us why. They give us warnings, cautions and helpful hints about alternative things we can do. When they are finished, we have been effectively talked right out of our dreams. Bumblebees do not talk and neither should we. If we have a dream we want to come true, the only way to it is through it. We must take a chance, a risk and a leap. If we believe in ourselves and our ability, we will be taught how to fly.

I can do it because I believe I can do it.

If you can learn to be a hole in the wall, things will
happen through you, not to you.
– John Randolph Price

Nothing ever happens to a hole in the wall. Everything
passes through it. Things happen around it. Things happen
above it and below it, but the hole remains the same.
Even if the hole is covered, it remains; never losing its
identity, doing what it was created to do. Nothing gets
stuck in a hole in the wall. Everything comes into the
hole; nothing stays in the hole; the holes defines itself by
being a hole. Things come to the hole in the wall. Light.
Air. Darkness. Sound. It takes from everything that comes
and willingly allows everything to go. How would you
define a hole in the wall? Is it nothing? Is it everything?
Is it something? Is it all things? A hole in the wall cannot
be defined; therefore, it cannot be limited. You cannot
identify a hole in the wall; it has an identity all its own.
Is it a big hole? A small hole? A black hole? A white
hole? The only way to define the hole is based on how
you see it.

Today I Am a hole in life's wall.

24 May

You must structure your world so that you are
constantly reminded of who you are.
– Na'im Akbar

Your subconscious mind is a twenty-four-hour photographer, recording every item you see. It is important to your mental, emotional and spiritual health that the things you see create images in your mind of who you are or what you want to be. Your environment should reconfirm your identity and the things you want. Is your home peaceful? Orderly? Safe? Are there pictures and artifacts that reflect the images you aspire to live up to? Does your work environment promote your creativity? Does it foster healthy communication? Does it look like a place you want to be? Like to be? Need to be? Is your social environment relaxing? Are you with the type of people you want around you? Do your family and friends support you and make you feel welcomed? Important? Free? Or are you restricted? Oppressed? Unproductive? You can only live up to the images in your mind. Make sure that what you see does not keep you in a place you do not want to be.

My world promotes my growth and true identity.

25 May

Life has two rules: number 1, Never quit!; number 2, Always remember rule number 1.
– Duke Ellington

Life is going to be a challenge. There will be rough times, difficult situations, things to fall into, major obstacles, hurdles, stumbling blocks, forks in the road, knives in the back, mountains to climb, things to get over, oppositions to resolve, unpleasantness to face, feelings to understand, disappointments to accept, mysteries to solve, wonders to unfold and promises to keep to yourself. Now that you know what to expect, prepare yourself. Get ready. The only way to get to where you want to be is to do what needs to be done to get there. Do it fast. Do it slow. Do it right. Do it up. Do it in the daylight. Do it by the moonlight. Do it alone. Do it with others. Do it for free. Get paid to do it. Do it for yourself. Do it for the world. The moment you give up on doing it, it will never get done.

I Am doing it and doing it and doing it.

26 May

Everything that has happened had to happen.
Everything that must happen cannot be stopped.
– Dwayne Dyer

Everything that we experience, everything we think, feel and do is in divine order. It is part of the universal flow that helps us discover who we are. If our thoughts and emotions did not manifest as actions, how else would we see who we are? The world is not happening to us. We are happening to it. We are moulding it, shaping it, creating the good and the bad. Sooner or later we will get tired of what we are doing and will do something else. When we get tired of hate, we will stop living in fear. When we get tired of injustice we will stop judging one another. When we get tired of violence we will stop aggression in all forms. When we get rid of criticism, cynicism and victimization we will live in truth, take responsibility for what we do and stop blaming each other. When we get sick and tired of the chaos in the world perhaps we will begin to love our brother as we love ourselves.

I happen to be creating a better world.

No one can give you wisdom. You must discover it for yourself, on the journey through life, which no one can take for you.
– Sun Bear

There are so many wonderful secrets and sciences in the world we can use as tools to better our lives. Some of them have been hidden from us, others we have flatly rejected. We have rejected our own culture and traditions, yet without investigation we accept the world of others as truth. When we close any portion of our minds we close off a part of the world. Is it fear that keeps us locked in? Is it hopelessness? Or is it stubbornness? How can the descendants of genius be so closed to new information? How can the children of the first civilization be lost and hopeless? What will it take before we open our hearts and minds to the world that awaits us? What would our ancestors think if they saw us lost and struggling? Unable to do with so much more than they had.

Today I will open myself to another part of the world.

28 May

You must be willing to die in order to live.
– Yoruba proverb

Most of us have been taught that death is the ultimate end. Death is frightening; it is dark, the unknown, beyond our control. We resist death; we brace ourselves against it; we run away because we do not understand death merely means change. When single people marry, their single life dies. As people age, their days of youth are gone. Death is the prerequisite of change. When we become willing to change, we learn to accept death as a meaningful new beginning. We may never like the idea of death; it may never make us comfortable; however, when we want to change anything in life, we must be willing to face death.

I move peacefully through the darkness into the light of change.

29 May

You must do your own independent investigation
of truth.
– Baha'i teachings

Most of us believe only what we can see. Our eyes
limit us in our perception and experience of reality. Yet,
do we realize, whoever controls what we see or experience can, in fact, control our perceptions of reality? How
then can we determine what is truth and what is not?
We must investigate, we must probe. We must ask questions. We must seek. We must know truth intuitively, with
our hearts and minds in harmony. The moment we accept
what is given to us as truth, we lose our conscious reality.
We are living through the eyes of someone else. How can
we expect to find peace, harmony or self if we live through
the perceptions of another? We can't. Whether religion,
career, personal liberty or life itself, we must investigate;
we must seek. We must probe. We must ask questions.
We must be in charge of our own reality and know our
own truth.

I have a right to know.

30 May

I am the thinker that creates the thoughts
that create the things.
– Dr Johnnie Coleman

There are no circumstances around you more powerful than the power within you. You are responsible for your life through your consciousness. Racism, sexism, homophobia, ageism have no power over you unless you believe they do. A belief is the most contagious influence you possess. If you believe in circumstances, they can and will defeat you. If you believe in yourself, you are assured victory. There is a wonderful inner world at work within each of us. It knows no colour, gender or age. We fuel this inner world with initiative, ingenuity and a picture in our minds. The world responds and produces according to how we fuel it. If we picture poverty, oppression, failure, disease and doubt, we cannot expect to enjoy wealth, success and health. When we put the forces of our inner self to work with good thoughts, it will produce according to our system of ideas. If we can keep our inner world clean, fertilize our minds with productive positivity, the powers within will create, with dynamic force, all that we believe is possible.

Today I fuel my inner world with positive possibilities.

True power comes through cooperation and silence.
– Ashanti proverb

Have you ever heard the sun come out in the morning?
Did you hear the moon come out last night? Can you
demonstrate the sound made by the fusing of the sperm
and egg to create the miracle of life? We have been taught
in this society that power is loud, forceful, aggressive and
somewhat intimidating. It is not. In silence the Creator
works. His creations all appear in silence. In silence one
becomes attuned to the energies and forces that are unseen
and unheard. In silence one learns to cooperate. We must
cooperate with the flow of activity. In silence one learns
to bring the head and the heart into cooperation in order
to move with the strength and power of the forces in the
flow. Keep silent about your hopes and dreams. Cooperate
with yourself by doing only those things that will bring
them about. Be silent about what you are doing and when
you are doing it. Cooperate with those who will silently
support you. In the silence of the night, your dream will
come true and when the chatterboxes come to look for
you, you will be gone.

Silence is my best friend. I cooperate fully in
its presence.

1 *June*

Force against force equals more force.
– Ashanti proverb

There is nothing more infuriating than being in the presence of someone who makes a racial slur. Whether it is in the form of a joke, mindless comment or blatant disrespect, ignorance should carry no weight with you. The comment is a reflection of fear and shame. To respond means giving into fear and surrendering your power. Remember, what you focus your mind on will grow. When you allow yourself to be drawn into the ignorance of another, you will undoubtedly say or do something of the same nature. As hard as it may be, the best response is no response. In the silence of your comment, the sting of the words is sure to hit home.

I Am in charge of my words and deeds.

2 *June*

Nothing ever strikes without a warning.
– Danny Glover

Whenever we have a negative encounter, we wonder, 'How could they do this to me?' The reason is because you let them. Basic human nature makes us see people and situations the way we want them to be, not the way they are. We allow others to take advantage, manipulate, and in some cases, abuse us, because we don't want to 'believe' what our senses are telling us is true. We listen to the same old line, accept the same dead promises, follow them down the same road, in the hopes they have 'changed'. We listen to what they say and hear something else. We see what they do and turn our face. When the bottom falls out, we quickly place the blame for the pain on the other person. We shift our anger to them rather than accept our responsibility for the role we played. There are three keys to successful relationships: Never make anyone else responsible for your happiness; trust what your inner self feels, sees and says; and pay close attention to the warning signs.

I listen to what is said, not to what I hear.

3 June

Bad luck picks its company by invitation only.
– African-American folklore

For anyone who has ever said, 'My luck is so bad.' To those who have ever asked, 'Why do these things always happen to me?' For anyone who has dared to say, 'I give up!' Get a pencil, a piece of paper and write this down: What you ask for, you get. What you see, you are. What you give, you get back, someday, somehow, sooner or later. There is no such thing as bad luck. The ancient Africans said, 'With your own hands you make your success. With your own hands you destroy it.' We say things return to us. We do things we know are not good for us. We think things that create situations we don't want. The only way to create success or luck is to think, speak and act in ways that support ourselves.

I make my own luck.

4 *June*

Things don't just happen, they happen just.
– Dr Johnnie Coleman

When we face disappointments, challenges and obstacles, the first thing we ask is, 'Why me?' We don't always realize that things happen to us according to our dominant thoughts, words and deeds. Even when we work really hard to keep ourselves in a positive frame of mind, things happen. When events occur that we don't expect, they increase our faith, strengthen our ability to endure and bring forth our hidden talents, abilities and strengths. Why me? As Les Brown would say, 'Why not you? Would you like to recommend someone else?' Why you? Because you can handle it. Because you really do know what to do. Because you need a little nudge every now and then to keep you on or put you back on track. So the next time something happens to you, remember, things don't just happen. They happen the way they should, at just the right time, to the right people. Our job is to know we are equipped to handle it.

Divine order prevails in my mind and my life, right here, right now.

5 *June*

A new life will come forth from the womb of darkness.
– Na'im Akbar

Every new situation we face in life sends us back into the womb of darkness. Like an embryo, we must go through changes in order to become whole, healthy and complete. We may feel alone, confused or frightened. In reality, we are growing, developing, evolving. In the womb of newness, we learn what we can and cannot do, given the space we are in. Yet we must continue to stretch and flex as we grow. We come to acknowledge our limitations knowing they are temporary. There is eventually a way out. In the womb, we are nurtured, fed and protected by an unseen, unknown force. We are watched over and prayed for by the ancestors. They know what it is we must do. The womb is the place where we are strengthened and primed by the people we do not yet know. They are waiting for us to be born and share with them all the things we learned in the womb.

Out of this new darkness, there will come a light.

6 *June*

Give not that which is holy to dogs. Neither cast ye
your pearls before swine.
– Matthew 7:6

Should we wear our most expensive outfit to a mud
fight? Why then do we continue to place ourselves in
jobs, situations and relationships that ruin our peace,
health and self-value? Should we leave our most valuable
possession unguarded in a public location? Why then do
we place our minds and bodies in the reach of those
persons and situations with a demonstrated history of
abuse or neglect? We are, to ourselves, the most valuable
possession we have. Yet we waste our time, energy and
sometimes our lives in worthless situations among people
who are unworthy. We must value our ideas, our energy,
our time and our life to such an infinite degree that we
become unwilling to waste who we are. If we put on our
best and go to a mud fight, we can expect to get dirty.
If we place our head in the lion's mouth, we should expect
to get eaten.

I Am very valuable to me.

7 *June*

If you are on a road to nowhere, find another road.
– Ashanti proverb

When we are following the wrong teachings or philosophy, we get stuck. We do not evolve. Life just doesn't seem to come together. We see the same people saying and doing the same thing. We may all be in agreement, but we still are not growing. We may know there is something better, somewhere. We may want or need more. But because we don't know exactly what 'it' is, we stay stuck in what is familiar. Could it possibly be that it is time to move on? Shift gears? Get back to basics? Open our minds? Try something new? Well, we will never know until we try. The only way to really be sure we are on the right track is to derail ourselves for just a moment and see what new direction beckons.

I Am willing to make a change.

8 June

I am thankful for the adversities which have crossed my path and taught me tolerance, perseverance, self-control and some other virtues I might never have known.
– Anonymous

When we are faced with a problem, we seem ready, able and willing to do battle. Yet sometimes we enter the battle not being clear of the goal. The best way to ensure that we make it through the battle is to focus on the outcome, not on the war. Focus crystallizes and directs the powerful energy of the mind. Focus galvanizes the mental, emotional and physical energy to such an exact degree that our efforts cannot miss the mark. When we focus on the goal and not the obstacles that can and do come about, we ensure victory. We should not spend our energy worrying about what the 'enemy' might be doing. Like the mighty Ashanti, if we focus our thoughts, take our steps with confidence and move forward, we may stumble but we cannot fall. Focus gives the elk its grace. Focus gives the gazelle its speed. Focus gave the Ashanti strength and a tradition as undefeated warriors.

I remain focused on the goal, even in the midst of battle.

9 *June*

If rain doesn't fall, corn does not grow.
— Yoruba proverb

Every farmer knows a good hard rain is needed to make a healthy crop. It will strengthen the roots, fatten the stalks and produce a healthy yield. A responsible farmer prepares for rain. He prepares the field by clearing away all remnants of past crops. He irrigates the field so the rain water can run off. He carefully guards his crop to keep away the birds and insects. Through it all, he has faith in his ability as a farmer knowing he is doing all that he can. Our lives are much like a field of corn, our challenges are the rain. We don't mind planting the seeds, working the field or planning for the harvest, but we have a tendency to complain about the rain. If we focus our mind on the goals, we are putting on our raincoat and boots. If we cleanse ourselves of negative emotions, we are covered by an umbrella of strength. If we keep faith in ourselves regardless of what others say, we have all we need to weather the storm.

*The harvest I reap is measured by the attitudes
I cultivate.*

10 June

If you fall, fall on your back. If you can look up,
you can get up.
– Les Brown

When was the last time you watched a toddler learning
to walk? They take a few steps and fall. Then get up and
try again. Sometimes they bump their heads, bust their
lips or pull things down on to their heads. No matter.
They keep falling and getting up, until one day they make
it clear across the room. How did we lose that fierce
tenacity to make it no matter what? Most of us consider
ourselves much more capable than a toothless toddler, yet
they seem to have something we don't. The toddler seems
to know that it's okay to fall. They are always willing to
roll over, get up and try it again. A toddler who stum-
bles doesn't always fall. Stumbling actually moves them
ahead faster. A toddler will grab on to anyone or anything
until they get their balance. When they do, they let go
and move on. They don't seem to care how awkward
they look, whether or not people laugh at them or how
many times they fall. They do it over and over until they
get it right. Isn't it funny that those of us who know how
to walk are always afraid to fall?

I Am willing to do whatever it takes.

11 June

To be who you are and become what you are capable
of is the only goal worth living.
– Alvin Ailey

Life is not hopping from one mountaintop to another
because there is a valley between. At times, the valley is
a job you hate but need to feed the family. The valley
might be a failing or toxic relationship. The valley could
be a child who goes astray or a friend who betrays you.
The valley could be an illness or the death of a loved
one. The valley is dark, bleak, ugly and frightening. But
there is value in the valley. When you are in the valley,
you begin to muster the strength and power buried deep
within you. In the valley you begin to think, pray and
tap into your incredibly divine self. The valley gives you
a time to rest, to heal, to rejuvenate your being. It is an
opportunity to look up, to see and remember those
powerful mountain climbers who made it before you:
your grandmother, your hero, even yourself. You have
been in the valley before. Remember what you did, how
you got up and out. Let the thoughts and memories of
that success be the rope you use to pull yourself up.

I Am taking time to learn the value of the valley.

12 June

Most people think they know the answer. I am willing
to admit I don't even know the question.
– Arsenio Hall

Life is a series of mysteries we must each unravel at
our own pace. Our task is not to solve the mysteries but
to use them along our way. No one can tell us what is
good for us just because it worked for them. If we allow
someone to give us our answers we create conflict deep
within. Sometimes it gets confusing trying to figure out
what to do. If the confusion is on the inside, the answer
is there, too! No human being has all the answers, if they
did they would not be here. One of the greatest mysteries
we must unravel is our purpose, because that makes us
clear. Let us take more time to listen to our hearts, filtering
through the offerings that come in. Let us not be so
willing to say 'I know' when we have no idea where to
begin. Let us know deep down that God loves us and use
that knowledge along the way. Let us approach the great
mystery of the meaning of life with a little bit less to say.

I Am on the path to knowledge.

13 June

Power concedes nothing without a demand.
– Frederick Douglass

Have you noticed how long hard times seem to last? And don't rainy days seem to go on forever? Do life's difficulties appear to multiply rapidly? When hard times, difficulties or rainy days appear, do you give them all your attention? If you are like most of us, you probably do. And like most of us, you give difficulty power. Nothing is ever as it seems. What looks bad today, can be a blessing tomorrow. Challenges come so we can grow and be prepared for things we are not equipped to handle now. When we face our challenges with faith, prepared to learn, willing to make changes, and if necessary, to let go, we are demanding our power be returned.

My willingness to grow is my demand for power.

14 June

Predict Life's Alternatives Now

Plan. Do you have a plan? What is your plan? Have you failed to plan? Can you carry out the plan? If you do not have a plan, what do you plan to do? Life is much too precious to waste time on wonder and worry. You can predict your life's alternatives now, if you take the time to plan. Plan your moments to be joyous. Plan your hours to be productive. Plan your days to be filled with peace. Plan your weeks to be educational. Plan your months to be filled with love. Plan your years to be purposeful. Plan your life to be an experience of growth. Plan to change. Plan to grow. Plan to spend quiet moments doing absolutely nothing. Planning is the only way to keep yourself on track. And when you know where you are going, the universe will clear a path for you.

I plan to be all that I Am.

15 June

As soon as healing takes place, go out and
heal somebody else.
    — Maya Angelou

No man is free until all men are free. No woman is
healed until all women are healed. These are more than
profound statements worthy of thought. They are the
clues to the moral responsibility we all have for one
another. Many of us hold on to our pain, afraid to reveal
it. Ashamed to admit it. Others hold on to healing information because we believe it is ours to own. We may
fight for the freedom of people of colour, but we say
nothing when gays or women are oppressed. We owe it
to ourselves and everyone else to see that all people live
painless and free. It is our duty to share what we know
if it has helped us to move beyond some darkness in life.
We can talk it out or write it out, but we must get it out
to those in need. We can support someone and encourage
someone else to take healing steps or paths or ways. We
should think about where we would be if there were no
books or people to guide us when we need it. Then, with
an open heart and extended hand, we can pull someone
else along.

I Am a valuable tool in someone's healing process.

16 June

And He sent them out . . . to heal.
– Luke 9:2

We must realize that the healing power of spirit is within each and every one of us. We each have the power to heal not only ourselves, but our world and all those around us. Spirit expressing through us as a kind word, a caring touch or a simple smile may be all it takes. When we realize who we are, the blessings we have been given, the power we embody, we have tapped into the source of our healing ability. Every day we have at least one opportunity to help a friend, a loved one or even a stranger. Regardless of the colour of our skin, our economic status, our social or political philosophy, it is our responsibility to do what we can, when we can, to assure that someone else does better. Today, let us become aware of the healing power within and dedicate ourselves to uplifting those we touch.

Through the healing power of the spirit within, I bless others today.

17 June

Do not follow the path. Go where there is no path
to begin the trail.
– Ashanti proverb

It takes courage, strength and conviction to go against
the grain. But if someone hadn't done it, we wouldn't
have wheat bread, chocolate chip ice cream or radios in
our cars. It is often difficult to get other people to follow
your train of thought. Stop trying. It's your train. You
are the engineer and the conductor. We usually want and
need help, support and comfort when we are doing something new. If we do not get it, so what! Does it mean we
should stop what we are doing? Absolutely not! The path
to success is paved with road signs, warning symbols and
obstructions. But when you start a new trail equipped
with courage, strength and conviction, the only thing that
can stop you is you.

I Am a trailblazer.

No one can uproot the tree which God has planted.
– Yoruba proverb

When we think our enemy is gaining on us, we want to run and run. When we believe someone wants what we have, we squeeze the life right out of it. When we believe 'they' are out to get us, we find 'their trap' at every turn. Yet if we would just stop running, squeezing and suspecting, we would understand who 'they' really are. They are the thoughts that beat us down, causing us to behave in unproductive ways. They are the doubts and suspicions we carry within us, and take the life out of the very thing we want. They are the fears that we fall into, showing us the very thing we don't want to see. They are us when we don't have faith because faithlessness is the greatest enemy. No one can get what is meant for you. The universe will not have it the way is should not be. We have been put on this earth to be a certain way, have a certain thing, accomplish a certain task. Until we have been, done and had what we came here to be, do and have, we are the only ones who can get in the way.

What is mine is mine alone.

19 June

The main point in the game of life is to have fun.
We are afraid to have fun because somehow that
makes life too easy.
– Sammy Davis, Jr

We live in a world that thrives on fear. Fear of living, fear of dying; fear of having too much, fear of not having enough. When people find our weaknesses we become fearful of them. If we demonstrate our strength, people become fearful of us. Fear is an accepted way of life. We are fearful our past will be repeated. We are fearful that we have no chance in the future. We are fearful of one another. We are fearful of those who are fearful of us. When we allow fear to control our daily lives we run the risk of remaining where we don't want to be – in fear. We must confront the things we fear, people and situations, believing the spirit of God is with us. By doing the very thing we fear, we tap into a force that directs and protects us, unleashing the power that has brought us this far. When we give in to our fears and avoid taking chances, it is unlikely we will ever overcome the very things we fear.

As my sense of power increases, my fear about
life decreases.

20 June

And the earth was without form, and void; and
darkness was upon the face of the deep.
– Genesis 1:2

Are you afraid to face the darkness of something new?
Do you want to know everything right now and be able
to see what is before you? Well, just imagine if the Creator
had waited for a model to shape the world. Who? What?
Where would you be today? When facing the darkness,
have faith. Active faith works through you and for you.
When we approach something new, surrender. Surrender
your desire to be in control. It is the eagerness to know,
the desire to control and the inability to surrender that
creates fear. Remember, the same force that created the
world without a model is the substance upon which you
stand. Stand firm in the darkness knowing there is something solid there.

I surrender to the power of the divine within me.

21 June

Love is the light. Forward is the motion.
– BarbaraO

God is love, a presence who enters our lives the very instant we pass from the darkness of the womb to the light of the world. Birth is a forward movement from the known to the unknown. It is a forward thrust from the warmth to the cold. It is a journey from unknowing to knowing and to recognition of the light. God never asks us to move backwards. We are simply asked to grow. The love light of birth remains with us until the earthly task is complete. Then we move forward into the realm of the known. The source of the light. The cause of the love. No matter what situations we are given in life, the light of love is there. As long as we are in the light the movement must be forward. The more we love the greater the light. The greater the light the easier the birth.

In all situations, under all circumstances I will stay in the light.

22 June

Exploring the question brings more wisdom than
having the answer.
— *A Course in Miracles*

If you attack a problem, you are going to get your butt
whipped. Anything you attack will fight back. Chances
are, if you have a problem, it is bigger than you; it crept
up on you or you didn't know what you were doing in
the first place. Don't attack your problems. Face them,
confess them, understand what they are — that is the
process. The process teaches and brings a richness that
will help you avoid future problems. When you attack a
problem it means you want a solution. The solution is
not always the answer, but the process is. The process
keeps you in the moment and you must be in the moment
to fully experience the solution. When you wrestle, attack
or fight a problem you are focused on a place you are
not — the future. You are here, in the moment, exactly
where the problem is. So calm down, understand what
is really going on and then surrender to the process.

*Today I will not attack a problem, I will go through
the solution process.*

23 June

Self-hate is a form of mental slavery that results in
poverty, ignorance and crime.
– Susan Taylor

When you don't feel good about yourself, it is hard to
feel good about anything or anyone else. You see everything with a jaundiced eye. You miss the value and worth
of every experience. You limit yourself because you don't
feel good about who you are or what you do. You hold
yourself back because you don't believe what you want
is worthwhile. You put yourself in situations that are
abusive or unproductive. You feel bad about yourself
because of what you've done. Self-hate is a vicious cycle
that leads to self-destruction. It fills the world with hate
and people with despair. The only way to get out of the
cycle of self-hate is to allow yourself to believe the world
is waiting for who you are becoming. What the world
must do is let every being know they are appreciated and
welcomed simply for being who they are.

I Am loving myself for being a lovable being.

Males understand power by doing powerful things.
Females just understand power.
– Stuart Wilde

It was an ancient tradition in an African village that
the women choose the leaders. As time passed on, modern
ideas prevailed and the men refused to adhere to tradition. The men picked the new leaders and within nine
months the village riches had been sold, the temples were
invaded and 85 percent of the elders, women and children were killed. The symbol for male ♂ indicates an
outward action. It is aggressive. It must have something
to do. The symbol for female ♀ is downward and inward.
It is a container that receives what is done. If we are to
achieve the world balance and harmony we seek, men
must step back and honour and learn from women. If
we want to stop the aggression and destruction of the
world, women must individually and collectively honour
themselves.

*Today I will support, honour and respect
the feminine power.*

25 June

Six million women were abused in 1991. One in every six was pregnant.
– Sally Jessy Raphael

Abuse against women is more than a crime of violence. It is a statement about society's view of women and itself. Women have been viewed as property, tools of pleasure and underlings. The people who support these views forget that women are the mothers, daughters, aunts, sisters and nieces who raise the fathers, sons, uncles, brothers and nephews. Women are the creative force of the world. The world's treatment of women will be reflected in the things men create. Every man of colour has an ancestral obligation to get clear regarding his views about women. Childhood pains, adolescent disappointments, adult misconceptions must be mended and forgiven. Every woman of colour has a responsibility to all women of colour to reveal the violence against her, to heal her wounds and do everything in her power to make sure another woman is healed.

I Am every woman.

26 June

Advice is what we ask for when we already know
what the answer is, but wish we didn't.
– Erica Jong

Each of us is born knowing everything we need to
know. It is programmed in our genes. It is connected to
our mission and purpose in life. People of colour in
particular are genetically coded for genius. We are,
however, programmed to self-destruct. We are taught we
must be authorized, qualified and sanctioned by someone
else. Unfortunately, we believe it. We don't trust ourselves.
We search for the support and acceptance of others. We
question what we know unless we can identify someone
else who taught us. We forget we have a built-in mechanism of information, protection and guidance. We move
outside of ourselves, then lament when we get lost. If we
are to survive we must accept and understand what we
already know. The key issue becomes 'Do I have the
strength and courage to do what I know is right for me?'

I know that I know that I know I Am knowing.

27 June

The passion for setting people right is, itself, a dis-ease
with the self.
– Marianne Moore

Many of us have a need to be right. Usually this stems
from the inner cry, 'There is something wrong with me.'
We then set out to make ourselves right by making someone
else wrong. We may plan what to say. We may canvass
others to elicit their support. In some cases, we simply
attack, letting others know how wrong they are and why
we think so. Self-righteousness is an affliction. It is an
inner desire to be accepted and valued. It is a camouflage
for feelings of worthlessness. No matter how wrong
another may be, it will never make you right. Self-value,
self-worth and self-esteem cannot come as a result of
being the only right one. It must come from knowing
who you are from within and feeling good about it.
Europeans being wrong will not make African people
right. Women being wrong will not make men right.
White people being wrong will not make Native Americans
right. We must get right with ourselves. Once we do, we
will have so much to do, we will not have time to keep
track of who is wrong.

I'm okay, you're okay, now let's get to work.

28 *June*

Victory has a hundred fathers and defeat is an orphan.
– John F. Kennedy

People sure do remember when you do something that's out of line, out of character or just plain dumb. They have a way of letting you know how shocked, surprised or disappointed they are. There are even those times when someone will believe that you committed the error or mindless act just to strike out at them. They may want to berate, scold or chastise you, probably giving very little consideration to how you feel. You are probably beating up on yourself and do not need the help of others. But you get it and that's how the shame, guilt and anger set in. No matter what you do, you must never lose sight of the fact that it is your lesson. It does not matter what anyone else thinks or believes; you are the one growing and learning. You have nothing to feel guilty, ashamed or angry about, you must be ready for the lesson, otherwise you would not have had the experience. Rather than focusing on what 'they' are saying, identify what you have learned and remember how awful it felt to be criticized the next time you start to criticize someone else.

No one has to tell me what an important lesson I
am learning.

29 *June*

If you are not totally free, ask yourself, why?
– Stuart Wilde

White people like violins, Black people like drums. White people play bridge, Black people play blackjack. White people eat caviar, Black people eat pigs feet. White people play squash, Black people play football. People do not do what they do because of the colour of their skin. They do what is familiar to them, accessible to them and what vibrates in their soul. It's about ancestry. It's about tradition! It's about what feels good and what doesn't. And it's all okay. Once we begin to understand that we are so much more than colour, we can begin to accept our individual differences. We can eat what we want, play what we want, go where we want, do what we want – because we choose to. No one thing is better than the other because of who does it. What makes an activity attractive and available is how it is supported by the people who do it. Do what you do because you like to do it, not because your colour keeps you from doing something else.

It's a soul thing. You have to do it to understand.

30 June

One love. One heart. Let's get together and feel alright.
– Bob Marley

   True power, our power, is in our diversity and difference. It is not in the illusive power we chase in money and things. It is not in what we call unity. We are already unified through breath. We want to deny our unity because we look different, act different and we believe we want different things. The elk, oak and pine live together to create the mighty forests. The shark, dolphin and whales live together to create the wealth of the oceans. The blue jay, hawk and robin sing together to create the melody of the sky. The lion, elephant and jaguar live together in the wonderment of the wild. They all want the same things: food, protection for their young and the opportunity to move freely. The animals do not blame or judge. They live without anger or fear. Are the animals just stupid? Or have we become too smart?

Today I will honour and respect the power in difference.

OTHERS

1 July

The love we desire is already within us.
– *A Course in Miracles*

God is love. That is where we must begin. We cannot expect to have a loving relationship with our family, mate or children until we heal our individual relationship with God. In the ancient traditions of people of colour all life was centred around the Creative Force and its elements. Our ancestors had a wholesome respect for the Creator and all creations. They honoured the earth for support, the sun for the life force and themselves as expressions of creation. Today we relate to one another's ego. We want to please one another because of who we are or what we have. We hold people in awe; we want people to fulfil our needs; we demoralize ourselves and one another for what we believe is love. God is love. That's it! God does not give presents. God does not have needs. God does not argue. God does not make threats. God does not feel abandoned. God does not deal with rejection. The only thing God does is love you and that is the only reason you are here.

The only relationship I will seek today is a relationship with love.

2 July

Having begun in the spirit, are you now to be made
perfect by the flesh?
– Galatians 3:3

The most accurate measure of our worth is how much
we value ourselves. When we value who we are, we are
sure to draw to us others who value us as much. When
we are needy, deficient, lacking confidence and self-esteem,
we will find ourselves in situations and among people
that reinforce those views. The first step in building relationships is learning to value who we are. We cannot
convince others how wonderful and marvellous we are if
we do not believe it. We must first convince ourselves. If
we repeatedly find ourselves in situations where we are
treated badly, we are responsible, not the other person.
When we find ourselves in situations where we do not
feel wanted, we must have the courage and confidence
to leave. Our sense of worth must first come from within.
When we have that, we can expect those in our relationships will value us as well.

The wealth of my spirit is the light of my world.

3 July

You must have love in your heart before you can
have hope.
– Yoruba proverb

At a very early age, we are taught to depend on someone else for our basic needs. When we are bald, toothless and helpless, it should be that way. As we mature, we must learn to become self-supportive and self-loving. A balanced, productive being is one who learns love of self. Loving yourself has nothing to do with being selfish, self-centred or self-engrossed. It means that you accept yourself for what you are and that you are willing to put your best foot forward, even if the foot is big. Loving yourself means that you accept responsibility for your own development, growth and happiness. It means you set the standard for how you want to be treated. Loving yourself means accepting your strengths and weaknesses, making a commitment to work on building and correcting what needs to be done. When you love yourself, you pave the way for all you want and need to come to you at the right time in the perfect way.

I love me.

4 *July*

Forgive and you will be forgiven.
– Luke 6:37

Everybody has had someone who has 'done them wrong'. When someone hurts us, we want to hurt them back. We live with anger and thoughts of revenge. We want to see them suffer. We want them to feel what we have felt. We want them to know they can't get away with what they did. But they did get away if your anger keeps you stuck in the situation. When the table turns, we make mistakes, we create pain for others, and we cannot understand why they do not or cannot forgive us. Perhaps it is because there is someone we need to forgive. Forgiveness frees us from the pain of the past and moves us beyond our mistakes in the future. What you give you get. When you forgive, forgiveness is there for you if you need it.

I forgive everyone for everything, totally and unconditionally.

5 July

If you are willing to deal with the past, you can make
the moment you are in rich.
– Oprah Winfrey

We are products of our past, the environment of our
childhood. For those of us who had painful childhoods,
we are determined to get away from our memories. We
cannot. Our past is a part of our today. We carry it in our
hearts. We model what we saw, heard and experienced as
children. It is called a pattern. We do what was done to
us. We behave the way we saw others behave. Unwittingly,
with a great deal of denial, we repeat the physical, emotional
and mental patterns set by our families. The only way to
stop the cycle, to break the pattern, is to go back and deal
with the pain. We must relieve the memories before we
can erase them. We must confront the people in our minds
and say now what we could not say then. We must explore
the feelings, unpack the guilt and free ourselves from the
baggage we picked up at home.

The buck stops with me.

6 July

You cannot belong to anyone else, until you
belong to yourself.
– Pearl Bailey

Finding and beginning a new relationship can be difficult. It is particularly difficult when we are carrying baggage from past relationships. We are told that it is not good to carry past relationships into the current ones. You know that. But how do you free yourself from that which is a part of you? You don't! Yet you can unpack the baggage. You can take a look at the pain, guilt, fear. You can look it dead in the face and see what it is, for what it is – the past. It's over. Without shame, without blame, you must look at what happened and know it does not have to happen again. It is only when you refuse to look, refuse to release, that you will have experiences added to your baggage collection. There is another point you often forget when moving into a new relationship: No matter how painful the past has been, you made it through.

Today, I Am unpacking.

7 · July

Don't look back and don't cry.
– El-Hajj Malik El-Shabazz (Malcolm X)

Are you stuck in your first relationship? Your fifth? Your last? Most of us are stuck in the memory, ideals, pain or trauma of a past relationship. We hold everyone responsible for the things someone did to us in the yesteryear. We can't seem to put the baggage down, overcome the disappointment or forgive the past. And we can't figure out why we end up in a similar relationship, the identical situation or with a broken heart. What we draw to ourselves is what we are! If we are hurt, angry, in pain, confused, disappointed or lonely, we will attract mates who will bring more of what we already are. We can only draw to ourselves the beings on our ray. If our ray is dark and dismal we will attract our reflection. If we want to move beyond the pain of past relationships, we must stop crying about them. Stop thinking about them. Stop drawing them to us. Forgive, let go and move on. When we move beyond where we are, the past cannot follow.

I'm moving up, out and beyond.

8 July

To understand how any society functions you must
understand the relationship between the men
and the women.
– Angela Davis

What type of relationship did you have with your
parents? How do you really feel about them? Whatever
your relationship is or was with your parents will be
reflected in the types of relationships you have in your
life. It will be difficult for you to have a good relationship with women if you did not have a good relationship
with your mother. Whatever the image, thoughts and feelings you have about your father will be reflected in your
relationships with men. Your relationship with them is
your model of what to expect, what is and is not accept-
able. When the memories of our parents are disappointing,
frightening and/or painful, we may repeat these patterns
in our lives. We can break the pattern when we forgive
our parents. They did the best they could based on the
pattern and model they lived with. They have hurts and
pains and bad memories, just like we do. Our parents
are just people who did the best they could with what
they knew.

I forgive my parents and release their patterns.

A man is an idea in Divine Mind; the epitome of
being; the apex of creation.
– Charles Filmore

The following is a list of adjectives used by a group
of a hundred women to describe men. A man is: a dog;
a liar; irresponsible; unfaithful; hard to communicate
with; a good worker; strong; a pain in the neck; lazy;
sloppy; inconsiderate; unemotional; unreliable; not to be
trusted; cheap; a user; manipulative; hard to please; messed
up in the head; too aggressive; too possessive; confused
about what he wants; out to take advantage of women;
the only thing that can really hurt a woman; hard to love;
a good lover; a sex fiend; stupid; hard to catch; difficult
to keep; not worth the effort; a disappointment; a waste
of time; cute when he's sleeping; better off without a
woman; a joke; okay to his mother; too smart for his
own good; the last thing on my Christmas list.

Twelve of the women were in long-term, loving relationships. Sixty-three of the women did not know their
fathers.

*A man is a mind thing. Whatever is in my mind I will
find in a man.*

10 July

A woman is the intuitive perception of truth reflected
as love in the soul.
– Charles Filmore

The following is a list of adjectives used by a group of a hundred men to describe women. A woman is: a bitch; a liar; fickle; hard to please; a sneak; a credit wrecker; a pain in the ass; a mother; a helpmate; God's gift to man; weak; stupid; here to serve man; nothing without a man; a sexual object; a tease; something I don't want to have anything else to do with; spiritual; nice to have around; a tax deduction; greedy; a heartache; a heartbreaker; capable of anything low down and dirty; frightened; jealous; too mouthy; angry most of the time; confused; sweet; nice to look at; hard to handle; my mother; a fool; thinks she's smarter than men; my best friend; a gossipmonger; able to make it in the white man's world; a welfare recipient; too emotional; unsure of herself; the reason I work two jobs.

Forty-seven of the men were in long-term loving relationships. Eleven men loved and admired their fathers. Forty-three admired their mothers.

*A woman is a mind thing. Whatever is in my mind I
will find in a woman.*

11 July

Your divine mate is seeking you and you can only
meet divinely.
– Jewel Diamond-Taylor

Your divine mate already exists. You are being prepared
to meet one another. Through your many growth experiences, and the purpose that is etched in your soul, the
day will come when you will meet face-to-face. It will be
crystal clear that this person is the right one. She will not
need fixing. He will not require work. You will be touched
in a place in your heart and soul that, until that divine
day, has been untouched. As you allow yourself to accept
the reality that your divine mate exists, it will unfold as
a reality to you. You can stop looking, forcing and trying
to make it happen. You need not fret or worry or allow
yourself to be lonely, because your divine mate already
exists. You can stop looking out for him or her. Instead,
spend your time looking within. When you get to the
place in yourself that is peaceful divine love, your true
mate will be revealed.

*My divine mate will be revealed to me in the divine
way at the divine time.*

12 July

If you are having a bad day, get another one and
get it quick!
– Rissie Harris

If you are having a bad day, it is a personal problem the world does not have to deal with. If you get up on the wrong side of the bed, it is no one's fault but your own. If it is that time of the week, month or year for you, what would you have the world do? It is never an excuse for being rude, cruel or abusive to anyone, to simply say, 'I am having a bad day.' It is not appropriate to scream, swear, lash out or do things that have no place among civilized people because 'you have something else on your mind'. We cannot abuse or traumatize others because we are facing a challenge. *LIFE IS A CHALLENGE!* African tradition tells us that it does not matter what difficulties we face. Our worth is measured by how we face those difficulties. If we are to grow and reach our fullest potential, we have no time to waste on bad days.

Today is a new day. I refuse to get off to a bad start.

13 July

The ruin of a nation begins in the home of its people.
– Ashanti proverb

If you have an argument at home, chances are you will have one at work. If you feel unsupported at home, your friends are likely to abandon you. If you are uncooperative, unreliable and disrespectful at home, you carry that same energy everywhere you go. Home is the foundation of everything we see and do in the world and relationships. For people of colour, culture mandates that one make home the primary concern of the heart. The heart creates love, support, cooperation, nurturing and peace. Home is our first school. Let us put our hearts, minds, bodies and souls back into the home as the first step toward eliminating the violence in the streets.

My home is my salvation.

14 July

The needle pulls the thread.
– Yoruba proverb

When we make strides in life we face obstacles and challenges. There are times when that which is most familiar to us will present the most challenging opposition – our family. If our life moves away from what is familiar to our family, they become frightened we will leave them. They may use their fears and concerns as a reason not to support us. They may not understand why we cannot do things the way they've always been done. The way they are comfortable with doing things. We want our family to support and encourage our dreams, but if they don't, it is okay. Sometimes we must step out alone, make a new way, start the path others will follow. Our job is to let our families know that we love them, keep them as informed as they care to be; when possible, we should invite them to join us in the process. However, if they choose to stay on the same old beaten path, there is no obligation to march with them.

I am weaving the fibres of a new world.

15 July

People come into your life for a reason, a season or a lifetime. When you figure out which it is, you know exactly what to do.
– Michelle Ventor

Wouldn't it be wonderful if our first love could be our one and only love, forever and ever, amen? Well, surely you know by now that life is not like that. People come and go in our lives, taking a little piece of our heart with them. As difficult or painful as it may be, that is exactly what they should do. We have more than enough love to share and spare, and we should give it freely. When we love for a reason it feels good to give love, because we get what we give. When we have a seasonal love, it is a whirlwind love, preparing us for something better. When those very special people come into our lives, we can and do love them forever. Loving is not what causes our emotional damage, it is the attempt to throw people out of our hearts and minds. When we love reasonably for the season we are in, we will undoubtedly enjoy a lifetime of loving.

I know why you are in my life and I love you for that reason.

16 July

A reason . . .

When someone is in your life for a reason, it is usually to meet a need you have expressed outwardly or inwardly. They have come to assist you through a difficulty, to provide you with guidance and support, to aid you physically, emotionally or spiritually. They may seem like a godsend, and they are. They are there for the reason you need them to be. Then, without any wrongdoing on your part or at an inconvenient time, this person will say or do something to bring the relationship to an end. Sometimes they die. Sometimes they walk away. Sometimes they act up or out and force you to take a stand. What we must realize is that our need has been met, our desire fulfilled; their work is done. The prayer you sent up has been answered and it is now time to move on. Next!

When a prayer is answered, there is no need to cry.

17 July

A season . . .

When people come into your life for a season, it is because your turn has come to share, grow or learn. They may bring you an experience of peace or make you laugh. They may teach you something you have never done. They usually give you an unbelievable amount of joy. Believe it! It is real! But only for a season. In the same way that leaves must fall from the trees, or the moon becomes full and then disappears, your seasonal relationships will end at the divinely appointed time. When that time comes, there is nothing you can say or do to make it work. There is no one you can blame. You cannot fix it. You cannot explain it. The harder you clutch, the worse it will feel. When the end of a season comes in a loving relationship, the only thing for you to do is let go.

For everything there is a season.

18 July

A lifetime . . .

Lifetime relationships are a bit more difficult to let go of. When a parent, child or spouse is involved, the wounds are very deep. When the end of a lifetime relationship comes, you may feel that you would be better off dead. The pain seems to grow, the memories linger, a part of your life is dying. You relive every painful moment in an attempt to understand. Your job is not to understand. You job is to accept. Lifetime relationships teach you lifetime lessons; those things you must build upon in order to have a solid emotional foundation. They are the most difficult lessons to learn, the most painful to accept; yet these are the things you need in order to grow. When you are facing a separation of the end of a lifetime relationship, the key is to find the lesson; love the person anyway; move on and put what you have learned to use in all other relationships.

A new life begins when a part of life ends.

19 July

The most frightening part of helping is getting involved.
– Dianne Ridley Roberts

With all that goes on in our daily lives, we may believe we don't have time to get involved with other people and their issues, yet we must. Perhaps we think if we do not see or hear about the problems, they will go away, but they will not. People of colour are a communal people. That means the community is our lifeline. African, Latin, Native American and Asian cultures are cultures of 'we' not 'I'. We cannot consider ourselves free, prosperous, successful or at peace as long as anyone who looks like us suffers. We cannot help everybody, but you can help somebody. We cannot do everything, but you can do something. If we each participate in a cause, if we each battle an ill, if we each contribute time or money to someone for something, a great deal could be done. If we each shoulder a bit of the responsibility for us, we can progress faster.

I will do my part for us.

20 July

Someone was hurt before you; wronged before you; hungry before you; frightened before you; beaten before you; humiliated before you; raped before you; yet, someone survived.
– Maya Angelou

What do you do when it seems as if people want to stay in their pain? They have a story to tell and they tell you every chance they get. It may get to the point that they become so entrenched in their pain that they stop looking for a way out. Well, believe it or not, they may like where they are. Our job is to leave them there. You can point the way out of pain, but you cannot force them to get out. You can support the move beyond their limitations, but you cannot make the move. Movement requires learning from painful experiences by recognizing the role we have played. If we continually tell the story without drawing a conclusion, we become the victims of the drama of the pain.

You can do anything you choose to do.

21 *July*

No person is your friend who demands your silence or
denies your right to grow.
– Alice Walker

   Have you ever wondered why people hide their dirty
laundry in the closet of your mind? Somewhere deep inside,
you may feel honoured when you are entrusted with
another's downside. What you fail to realize is that knowledge creates responsibility. When you are asked to remain
silent about the secret or hidden acts of another, you are
lured into collusion. If people demand your loyalty, presence or participation in that which is detrimental to them,
you create a detriment for yourself. When you abandon
your dreams, swallow your truth, give the will of others
precedence over your own, you sell yourself out. Be aware
of the person who asks you 'not to tell anyone' the thing
they cannot keep to themselves. Be responsible to yourself and let them know.

You are talking to the wrong person.

22 July

It goes without saying that your friends are usually
the first to discuss your personal business
behind your back.
– Terry McMillan, from *Mama*

If there is anything you don't want people to know
about you, don't tell anyone. We give people too much
responsibility when we entrust them with our business.
Sometimes they repeat the information mindlessly; other
times they use our story to make a point. We should only
tell our problems to people who can help. Eighty percent
of the people we talk to can't help us; the other 20 percent
really don't care. We are quick to accuse our friends of
betraying us, but do we consider how we betray ourselves?
We lie to ourselves and on ourselves and then allow
ourselves to believe it will not come back. It does, through
the mouth and actions of someone else. In those special
times when you must talk about your private affairs, ask
the other person if he is willing to keep your confidence.
If he repeats it, then the responsibility is his – not for
telling your business, but for not keeping his word.

I will only tell you what I want everybody to know.

23 *July*

Two men in a burning house must not stop to argue.
– Ashanti proverb

It is not your duty or responsibility to change the minds of other people. The nature of their thinking is advanced or limited by their experience. In your presence, they have an opportunity to learn about you and, perhaps, to grow. Allow them to experience you as a well-grounded, compassionate being who is capable of listening, learning, sharing and growing. That is your responsibility to yourself, your life and the other person. You can be an example of the peaceful, vibrant, valuable contributor your ancestors were. Like them, you can contribute to the enlightenment of the world when you spend less time worrying about what others think and more time creating positive change.

Every experience is an opportunity to grow.

24 July

Offensive words that come from your mouth, if
repeated, can make bitter enemies.
– *The Husia*, translated by Dr Maulana Karenga

Every mouth has two lips. The high lip gives to praise,
the low lip gives to gossip. When we do not guard what
we say or to whom we say it, we can never be sure which
lip will repeat the words. The ancient Egyptians gave
warnings about the unguarded movement of the mouth.
They understood the destructive potential of words on
the wrong lips. We may not be familiar with those ancient
teachings, but we do know the impact of low-lipped
speaking. Speak highly of everyone or say nothing at all.
Repeat only that which you have a duty to repeat and
repeat it with a noble intent. If something you say comes
back the wrong way, correct it immediately. If you quarrel
with family or friends, speak to them directly. Temper
your words with a consciousness of empathy. Speak the
way you would want to be spoken to. Remember that
your parents gave you the blessing of lips; speak to them
with an attitude of gratefulness.

I have spoken truly and done it righteously.

25 July

No investigation. No right to speak.
– Confucius

Very often we find ourselves involved in conversations of the 'he said, she said' variety. We may not know the parties involved or we may have heard some other version of the same story from another source. The sad thing is we use this information as the basis for our opinions and interactions with the people involved. There's an old African saying, 'Ears don't pass head,' which means we should never let what goes into our ears override good common sense. Common sense tells us we should accept people for who they are based on our individual experience with them. All too often the side of the story that is not told is the other person's side. It is in our best interests to give everyone a fair start, regardless of what we have heard about them. We should make our own mental inventory, identify any negative experiences we have had. If there are none, we should commit ourselves to be open and deal with people as they deal with us.

I am willing to give everyone a fresh start.

26 July

No one can judge you unless you let them.
– Swami Nada Yolanda

Don't 'should' on other people and don't let them 'should' on you. Should is a judgment we make based on our experiences and perceptions. When we pass that on to other people, we are judging them. Should is an expression of fear. It says that our way is the right way; if you move beyond that, you might prove I am wrong. Should is the way we control others, to make them think or behave the way we want them to. Should takes us on a guilt trip and limits our capacity to grow. If we only do the things we should do we will never learn another way we could do it. Should limits us to what is comfortable. Should keeps us in a place that is familiar. Should makes us responsible to someone other than ourselves when we know that is not the way we 'should' live.

I 'should' do only those things that feel right for me.

27 July

What is the quality of your intent?
– Thurgood Marshall

Certain people have a way of saying things that shake us at the core. Even when the words do not seem harsh or offensive, the impact is shattering. What we could be experiencing is the intent behind the words. When we intend to do good, we do. When we intend to do harm, it happens. What each of us must come to realize is that our intent always comes through. We cannot sugarcoat the feelings in our heart of hearts. The emotion is the energy that motivates. We cannot ignore what we really want to create. We should be honest and do it the way we feel it. What we owe to ourselves and everyone around is to examine the reasons of our true intent.

My intent will be evident in the results.

28 July

Each time we have sex we must be innocent and open.
– Ebun Adelona

Sexual intercourse is an act of profound creation. It is the meshing and weaving together of the Mother/Father force of the Creator. Whatever we hold in our heart the Mother and our mind the Father, during the sexual act will be created in our lives. Sex in anger will create angry words and angry situations that must be resolved. If we are in denial about ourselves, who we are or who our mate truly is in our life, then sex will create denial in the relationship. Sex in self-sacrifice will create a doormat. Whoever makes the sacrifice will be walked on. Sex in confusion creates chaos and more confusion about how and why we want sex. Unconscious sex, doing it just to be doing it, creates a violation in the subconscious mind. When we create children during misguided intercourse, the child brings to life the state of our being at the time of the act. We can heal and strengthen ourselves during our conscious sexual activity, but we must know what we are doing and why.

Sexual intercourse is a creative expression in which I fully participate.

29 July

Instant intimacy is very often followed by
desperate disillusion.
– May Sarton

We can become so emotionally charged by a person
that we allow ourselves to be intimate before we know
who the person really is. When we give our bodies to
another being, we are giving them a piece of our souls.
We might want to take the time to find out if they deserve
it. Sexual activity is not the only way to let someone
know we like them. Sharing information, supporting each
other's goals, giving of our time and energy without
expectations sends a much stronger message than sex. We
must take time to know the other person; understand
what they want, where they are going and figure out if
we want to be in the same place. When we let down our
hair too early in the game we are apt to end up with a
messed up head.

I will choose time over intimacy.

30 July

Everything, even darkness and silence has its wonders.
— Helen Keller

A history of abuse and labelling has created a tremendous strain on the sexual consciousness of people of colour. The ancestral memory of being labelled as animals to be studded and bred has made us fearful of our sexuality. What we must accept and learn to understand is that we can be sexual and still be spiritual. Even in the abuses of the past, people of colour were capable of loving and sharing that love as a sexual expression. We prayed for our freedom and the safety of our lives, and we still made love. Although the abuses have changed, many of our fears have not. Right now, there are many people of colour who become anxious, nervous and uncomfortable in conversations about sex. We do it, but we hide it. We make jokes about it in private; we tell stories about it in secret; when it comes to talking and sharing openly about sex, we shy away. Try this. Sex is wonderful. Sex is good. I like sex. Sex likes me. But don't take my word for it; try it for yourself — with the lights on.

I Am free to be a sexual being.

31 July

Let them wait. And wait they do.
— Jackeé

All relationships are like contractual agreements. Each party expects to receive certain things. In our intimate relationships, sex is like a signature on the contract. Unfortunately, many of us sign the contract without reading the fine print. By the time we discover what kind of deal we are being offered, we are bound by our signature. Some contracts have a ninety-day grace period. This gives the parties the opportunity to examine the merchandise, test the service, make any necessary adjustments or bow out of the agreement. It makes sense to apply a grace period to our intimate relationships. We may need time to assess behaviour, true intentions and the performance history of the prospects. The fine-print issues such as habits, motive and background cannot be seen with closed eyes.

I Am willing to read the fine print.

1 August

If you eat well, you must speak well.
– Yoruba proverb

When we become angry, upset or disappointed with someone, we forget the good they have done. We seem to think people must prove themselves to us again and again. If ever they fail to live up to our expectations, we are quick to voice our dismay. The ancient Africans taught that if a person is good to you, you must forever speak good of them. They believed the good always outlives the not so good. In order to keep the good flowing, you must speak of it. The ancestors taught that we must honour those who helped us when we were in need, regardless of what they do now. We must honour those who taught us, even if we no longer use the lessons. We must remember with a kind word the road someone else has paved for us, no matter where or how they travel now. Everything we receive in life is food for our growth. If we eat from the plate, we must give thanks. Remembering, without that food, at that time, we may have starved.

I remember only the good that has been done.

2 August

Go behind the apparent circumstances of the situation
and locate the love in yourself and in all others
involved in the situation.
– Mother Teresa

The moment we have a negative experience we get
stuck in what was done and how it was done to us. We
must learn not to take life so personally. People are not
really out to get us. Events are not waiting to befall us.
We are all moving to get where we want to be. As a
result, we will sometimes step on each other's toes. When
we find ourselves in a conflict or confrontation we must
know how to love ourselves out of it. Love means recognizing fear as an operand condition that sometimes makes
us do and say things we really don't mean. Love means
opening our hearts and minds to our best, regardless of
what is going on. Love means not attacking but supporting,
not defending but seeking clarity. Love means knowing
that, in the end, we will all be okay even if it means we
have to give up a little of something. Let us learn to give
up anger and fear by replacing those things with love.

I Am loving you and me out of this situation.

3 August

Each of us is stamped with vibratory signature of our
own state of consciousness.
– Paramhansa Yogananda

We become very offended if someone says we don't
measure up or if they criticize our actions. We think they
are picking on us because of our race, gender or because
'they' have a problem. We must consider what they are
actually saying before we dismiss what could be valuable
criticism. Consider the things we think about ourselves:
'I'm not good enough,' 'I'm not smart enough,' 'I didn't
do it right,' 'So and so did it better than me,' 'I need
someone to tell me how good I am,' 'I hope I don't mess
up, like I did before,' 'If I do it like this, they will like
me,' 'I don't know what I'm doing,' 'I'm not good at
this,' 'I can do better than this.' Life is an accurate reflection of our consciousness. People will usually say to us
the very things we think to ourselves. If we want others
to speak well of us, we must first think well of ourselves.
The next time someone criticizes you, think, 'Where have
I heard that before?'

I think positively about me and speak positively to me.

4 August

If you love 'em in the morning with their eyes full of crust; if you love 'em at night with their hair full of rollers, chances are, you're in love.
— Miles Davis

When was the last time you were in love? Really in love? Do you remember feeling silly? Giggling and grinning whenever you saw the object of your affection? Did you feel like skipping, running, jumping in the street? Maybe spinning around and rustling your hair? Did everybody look better, act nicer, seem beautiful because you were in love? What about playing? Didn't you want to stay home and play with your love mate rather than go to work or school? And didn't you want to go to bed early? Do you remember getting dressed up and wanting to look nice because you felt so good? Did you feel as if you could do anything because you had somebody at your side? What about feeling nurtured, supported, protected? How about being needed, wanted, valued? And didn't it bring a smile to your face just to think that somebody loved you? Did it make you feel young again? Well then, why do you think children don't know when they're in love?

Loves come to all ages.

5 August

I wish I woulda knowed more people. If I woulda
knowed more, I woulda loved more.
– Toni Morrison, from *Beloved*

We have an unlimited capacity to love. Actually, loving
is not something we do to or for other people. It is a
blessing, a gift we give to ourselves. Love opens us to
endless possibilities. It increases our resources and our
capacity to give. Love fine-tunes our vibrational frequency,
which enables us to create. Love keeps us alive long after
we have departed and gives meaning to who we are, what
we do and how we do it. The only thing that limits our
capacity to love are the conditions we place on loving.
When love is based on what we get or how we get it,
our love ability is stunted. When we love under circumstances rather than in spite of them, our love is limited.
When we love what was rather than what is, we have no
real idea what love is about. When we love just for the
sake of it, giving who we are without excuses or apolo-
gies, taking what comes and making the best of it, we
open our souls to the abundant blessings of the strongest
forces of life.

*Today I will pour love into everyone and
into everything.*

6 *August*

We are each born with a limitless capacity for pleasure
and enjoyment.
– Sondra Ray

Relationships do not just happen. No matter how we
meet our mate or who makes the introduction, we create
all the relationships we experience. We each have the
capacity to bring to ourselves the exact relationship we
want. Unfortunately, most of us are not willing to do the
work. We must begin the work by looking at the 'self'
and getting clear about how it feels. We cannot expect
to attract a loving, generous mate if we are angry and
withholding. We must stop blaming the past for our
condition now. Wherever we are, what we have or don't
have is no one's fault but our own. If by chance someone
else made a contribution to the mess we were creating,
forgive them the mess and move on. Finally, we must give
thanks for all we have been; all we have had; all we are
becoming. When we take the limits, restrictions and fears
off our hearts, our cup of love will run over.

I will look at me before I look for love.

7 *August*

Your mate is your mirror.

Many of us think we are lucky or blessed when we find just the right person to love. By now we know that nothing in life is an accident, including our selection of a mate. The people who come into our lives are a reflection of who we are. They reveal to us those things we cannot or refuse to see about ourselves. The very thing we don't like about our mate is the thing we need to change. The thing we love about the other person is a hidden, undeveloped or unrecognized asset that we have. We can only draw to us those people who are on our ray, our level of energy and development. They reflect back to us the very things we do. Most of us reject this idea. But then most of us reject criticism, too. We find it difficult to accept those things about us that others see. We do, however, feel completely justified when we criticize our mates. Here's a question for you: How would you know what to call what you see in your mate unless you had seen it somewhere else?

I am looking in the mirror of self and making adjustments in me.

8 *August*

The person who seeks to change another person in a
relationship basically sets the stage for a great
deal of conflict.
– Wesley Snipes

Very often we go into relationships with the idea that
we can make somebody better. We see their flaws or
shortcomings and take it upon ourselves to help them fix
what is wrong. Our task in our relationships is not to
fix one another. Our job is to love what we see and
support one another in doing better. Fixing is telling what
is wrong, why and how to fix it. Supporting is allowing
us to make our own choices, being there if things go
wrong and supporting us in doing better next time. Fixing
is forcing us to do it their way when our way doesn't
work. Supporting is sharing with us their needs and trusting
we will take them into account. Fixing is nagging.
Supporting is nurturing. Fixing is anger when things get
rough. Supporting is knowing things will get better.
Supporting is seeing us exactly as we are. Fixing is seeing
in them what we refuse to see in ourselves.

I love and support you exactly as you are.

9 *August*

Only choose to marry a woman whom you would
choose as a friend if she were a man.
– Joseph Joubert

We often have such unrealistic expectations of our mates
that it is as if we do not want them to measure up. We
want them to be like, act like, behave like some ideal-
istic model we have cooked up in our minds. The problem
is that we never reveal to them what the model is. We
hold them accountable and responsible to satisfy our
desires, but we forget to tell them what our desires are.
We must remember that our mates are people. They are
not mind readers. We are asking for disappointment when
we do not share with them our expectations. We complain
to friends, compare them to family members; why not
talk to the one person who could probably help set things
right? We should talk to our mates as if they are our
friends. Reveal to them those parts of us that we have
hidden from the world. And if in our heart of hearts we
cannot do this, we need to ask ourselves, 'Why am I with
this person?'

I want more than a mate, I want a friend.

10 August

If you know what you want, you will recognize it
when you see it.
– Bill Cosby

When we convince ourselves that we can't find the
right mate, we try to make the one we have into the one
we want. There are two ways to do this. First, we need
to see who we have and tell ourselves they are someone
different. The other way is to try and fix what we have.
Neither idea works. When we are not honest with ourselves
about who our mate really is, we end up disillusioned
and disappointed. It is not their fault, it is our own. We
must be clear about what we want from a relationship
whether it is social, business or intimate. Then we must
make a decision to wait for exactly what we want. If
who we have is not who we want, say so! It is not our
job to change the other person. If we buy a pair of shoes
and they do not fit, should we wear them and suffer or
take them back to the store?

Who I want is important enough for me to wait for.

11 August

Would you marry you?

We are always looking for the perfect relationship. The goal is to find that perfect someone who will make our lives a better place to be. It is unfortunate that we don't realize perfection runs two ways. In order to find that perfect somebody, we must believe that, whatever perfect is, we have already achieved it. No one can give us what we don't already have. Mr or Ms Right cannot be to us what we are not. If we are unhappy, unfulfilled, not pleased about who we are, we owe it to ourselves to stop looking. We have to ask ourselves: Would I marry me? Am I doing my best, giving my all, being the best I can be to myself? If not, why are we pawning ourselves off on someone else? We need to take time to do some homework on self-love, self-esteem and self-confidence. When we can pass the test of self-acceptance, the perfect someone who will complement all that we already are will walk right through the door.

The love and harmony within me reaches out and draws my mate.

12 August

Do not envy the oppressor, and choose none of
his ways.
– Proverbs 4:31

When someone does you harm, it seems only natural
that you should do the same to him, right? Wrong! You
can never get even with someone who has harmed you.
Any attempt to do so puts you behind the eight ball, again.
Two wrongs never make a right. Nor can you right a
wrong by committing another wrong. You may be able to
justify your actions politically or socially, but spiritually
you will be held accountable for what you do – why you
do it doesn't count. The pendulum of life swings both ways
and brings rewards at both ends of the spectrum. If you
use your mind, time and energy to cause harm to anyone,
the pendulum will sooner or later move in your direction.
If your slate is clean, when it swings toward you, you will
not have to worry about being knocked down.

*I settle all of my scores in the court of
universal justice.*

Let go!

When we believe we are losing control, we grab on tight. If we want to avoid pain, we hold on for dear life. When we are in fear of losing, looking bad or being abandoned, we tighten our grip. When our greatest fear comes upon us, we clench our fist and teeth, close our eyes and hold on. We must learn how to let go. We have the capacity to live through any adversity if we simply let it go. We cannot stop time or destiny. Whatever is going to happen has already happened; we must learn how to see it through to the end. When we hold on, we prolong the pain. When we dig our feet in, we must be uprooted. When the time comes for growth and change, we must have the courage and faith to let go.

Whatever leaves my life makes room for
something better.

14 August

If you cannot find peace within yourself, you will never find it anywhere else.
– Marvin Gaye

Where do we get the idea that if a relationship or a marriage ends, we have somehow failed? The ending of a relationship is not a sign of personal failure. Actually, it is a courageous step. It is a loving gesture. It is a responsible move. It takes courage to admit when a relationship is not working. When we are locked in a relationship that is not working, it can be very painful. We must love ourselves and our mates enough not to want them to stay in a situation that is causing pain. When we are willing to take personal responsibility and the necessary steps to free ourselves from the pain of a relationship, we are showing a willingness to grow. Looking at things from this perspective, how can we consider ourselves failures? There comes a time in every situation when difficult decisions must be made. Making the decisions may make us feel miserable; not to make them is what makes us miserable failures.

I am not a failure. I am ending a relationship.

15 August

Rejection can be killing. It kills faster and more
effectively when the victim is already lacking
in some vital way.
– Patti Austin

Nobody likes being rejected, but rejection does not
mean there is something wrong with you. An early rejection can save you a great deal of grief later on. Then
there are those times when what you have is not really
what you want, but you convince yourself to settle for it
anyway. Well, if the other person rejects you, you are
saved from having to run away. Rejection is only damaging
when you start out believing you are not complete. When
you enter a relationship needy and unfulfilled, rejection
can be a damaging blow. In those situations you must
not shrink away feeling defeated and afraid; you must
ask what is it that this person has, and why you don't
think you can get it anywhere else. If you understand that
you can only draw to yourself what you already are, you
can see rejection in another light. When you enter any
relationship, you want to be and feel the best you can.
If you get rejected, it might simply mean you have a little
more work to do.

When I accept me no one can reject me.

16 August

No one can see their reflection in running water. It is
only in still water we can see.
– *The Wisdom of the Taoists*

Divorce or separation following a long-term relationship creates many feelings. One of the strongest is 'something is wrong with me'. If your mate becomes involved
with another person or gives what you consider an unacceptable reason for moving beyond the relationship, the
feelings of inadequacy deepen. Why? What did I do? How
could you do this to me? Somewhere in the process you
lost sight of the fact that people have a right to change
their minds. You may not want them to do it. You probably won't like it when it happens. But people have a
right to change their minds and it has absolutely nothing
to do with you. Time marches on. People change. As people
change, their needs change. When people have a need, it
is their responsibility to themselves to see their needs are
met. And it has absolutely nothing to do with you.

There is nothing wrong with me.

17 August

Spend time alone in objective thought as you consider
the direction of your life.
— *I Ching* (*The Receptive*)

The entire purpose of life here on earth is for people
to be free. Why then do we spend so much time acquiring
things to make us comfortable and tie us down? Our
possessions keep us in bondage to jobs, debts, situations
and conditions. We spend precious time fighting with one
another as to the right way to fight for the freedom we
want. Women want to be free. We sit idly as men control
the markets, industries and services that are essential to
our survival. Women complain that men oppress them,
yet at the same time they believe the things men say
women cannot do. Men say they want to be free. The
average man spends his average day watching someone
else, wondering what someone else is doing, believing
someone else is waiting for an opportunity to take what
he has. What's the matter with these pictures? We will
never be free as long as we need something or someone
else to give it to us. Freedom is a state of mind not a
tangible condition.

I surrender everything to my freedom.

You have to love enough to let go.

There are times when loving someone means we must let them go. It is not healthy or productive to remain in a relationship that makes us happy sometimes, sad most of the time. Yet we hang on. We hang on believing that something bad will happen to the person if we let him or her go. That is our ego telling us what we want to hear. We hang on in fear that no one else will love them or us the way we want to be loved. This time the ego is telling us that we are not good enough. We hang on because we don't know who or what may come along. We believe there is a lack of available mates. We hang on wishing, hoping, trying to make it work – afraid it will not. When a relationship is over, it is over; but the love can live on. Loving someone means you want him or her to be happy. If that person can be happy without you, love enough to let go.

I know when to let go.

19 August

Friends borrow your books and sit wet glasses on them.
– Edwin Robinson

Sometimes the people we care about the most are the people we treat badly. We don't always mean to or want to. At times we just don't think. Other times we do it because we know we can get away with it. We must learn to value and honour those blessings we call friends; they are few and far between. They come to share a part of life with us. How we treat them is a reflection of our thoughts about life. When we tax our friendships with abuse, neglect or mindless actions, we shut ourselves off from the support that makes life easier to bear. When we fail to nurture our friendships, it is a sign that we do not nurture ourselves. When we treat our friends with kindness and respect, they are obliged to do the same. When we hold our friendships in high regard, we learn to feel good about ourselves. When we value our friends and the relationship, they know it, and they will do their best to keep things in balance.

I will treat my friends as well as I treat myself.

20 August

It is said that love is blind. Friendship, however, is clairvoyant.
– Phillipe Soupault

A friend, a real friend, someone you love and trust, is going to tell you all the things you do not want to know about yourself. A friend tells you when you are right and helps you understand how you could be wrong. A friend will yell and scream, but when you need him, he is there. A friend is someone you cannot and do not lie to. She knows your secrets and holds them in confidence. A friend never judges, yet will let you know when you are doing it 'again'. A friend sees your mistakes and, without covering them up, steers you in another direction. A friend pushes you, shoves you and drives you real hard. Just when you think you are about to break, he whips out the Band-Aids, patches you up and starts pushing again. A friend always says things that make no sense until you hear a stranger say the same thing. A friend is someone you can look at and see yourself and know you are really going to be all right.

When I see my friend, I see myself.

21 August

I was secure enough in my relationships with my
children that I did not have to fight my mother
for power.
– Gladys Knight

Mothers and daughters have many hurdles to overcome. There's the mother's view, the daughter's view. There's
the mother's opinion, the daughter's opinion. There's the
mother's fear that the daughter will not succeed. There's
the daughter's fear that she will not be supported in what
she wants. There's the mother's incessant nagging to do
things the 'right way'; there's the daughter's view that the
mother's way will not work. There are mothers who have
not grown up. There are daughters who have grown up
too fast. Then come the grandchildren, a chance for the
mother to do it again, better this time. Now there is a
way for the daughter to prove that the mother's way does
not work. The mother sees herself in the daughter – there
is pride and celebration. The daughter does not want to
be anything like the mother – there is disappointment and
embarrassment. Mothers and daughters reflect each other,
they repel each other, yet in spite of it all they love each
other. Sometimes they should tell each other.

I Am my mother's daughter.

22 August

We survived slavery because we held on to one
another. The moment we found independence, we
began to commit suicide.
— Dr Tesehloane Keto

There is a metaphysical principle that says whatever
we do to someone else, we actually do to ourselves. This
principle supports the golden rule 'do unto others'. We
forget this and when we do, we create an imbalance in
our own being. When we malign another person, we are
talking about the self. When we deal dishonestly with
someone, we are cheating the self. When we abuse, neglect
or abandon another, we are doing it to the self. Why?
Because we are connected by the one Creative source.
This source creates a responsibility for, accountability to
and dependence on one another. The moment we allow
the self to believe it can do without other people we create
the kind of loneliness, depression and disconnection that
makes life not worth living.

I Am one with the Source. I Am one with mankind.

Potential means – you ain't doing nothing now.
– Michelle Ventor

One of the greatest downfalls in our relationships is banking on the potential of someone else. We go to great lengths to understand what someone should do, could do, has the ability to do but is not doing. Very often what we see of the person prevents us from seeing that the person is doing nothing. Parents, friends and spouses have lost millions of dollars and valuable time saying, 'I see the good in you.' We usually want so much for our loved ones that we forget to ask what they want for themselves. You cannot want more for someone than they want for themselves. If they want it, it is up to them to go out and get it; you should not have to drive or take them to find it. Do not be concerned with what a person could do; pay close attention, listen intently to what they are doing and saying right now.

I see you in this moment.

24 August

Emotional independence begins with the development
of inner resources.
– Anonymous

We have been taught that a relationship is a fifty-fifty
proposition. A more accurate view is that two incomplete
people can come together and find completion. This is a
false premise that has had a disastrous impact on our
relationships. Each person must come into a relationship
a whole, complete person who is able to handle the responsibility; willing to share in the responsibility for mutual
growth. Fifty-fifty relationships usually do not work. The
premise is simple: What if both parties are missing the
same thing? A relationship must not be a crutch. We want
to develop complementary unions where strengths and
weaknesses have support. We want to be able to stand
on our own, but stand a little taller in a relationship. We
want to bring an identity to the table and have it reflected
to us a little brighter. In a relationship, two halves do not
make a whole, and we cannot allow anyone else to take
responsibility for our completion.

*I am bringing 100 percent of who I Am to
the love table.*

There is really a very little difference between people; it is called attitude; and it makes a really big difference. The big difference is whether it's positive or negative.
– W. Clement Stone

People are not always out to get you, but there are times when they do. Chances are the person was close to you – best friend, relative, parent, lover, child or spouse. There's an even better chance that you deeply loved and trusted the person. Perhaps they betrayed you. Abandoned you. Stole from you. Or failed to return the emotional commitment you made. No matter how traumatic the wrongdoing or end of a relationship may be, the good always outweighs the bad. If you have one bad memory, you have two positive ones. If you learned one new thing about yourself or another person, you know more than you did when you started. If you learned in this relationship what not to do in the next, you are better for it. If you learned patience, faith, trust, humility or what a truly strong and powerful person you are, you have treasures you will never lose.

The difference between me and them is I am positive.

It is your moral duty to be happy; however, you cannot exercise this duty by clutching unrealistic beliefs, struggling with unworkable assumptions, juggling painful images, jumping to false conclusions, running with impulsive decisions or massaging hasty judgments.
– Sufi Hazrat Inayat Khan

Too often we expect happiness to come as a result of our relationships rather than as a premise upon which to build one. If we truly wanted to be happy, we would not be so eager to sacrifice happiness for nonsense – jealously, possessiveness, anger, fear or any other function of the ego. Nonsense renders us downright miserable. Happiness requires that we be honest, trusting, trustworthy, respectful and mutually considerate. We cannot realize true happiness when we entertain nonsense in our hearts and minds. Individually and collectively, we must work to clear ourselves before entering a relationship. If we wait until we are in the process and wading through the nonsense, the ego will be well on the way to eroding the happiness we seek.

I will exercise my duty to be happy.

If you want to know the end, look at the beginning.
  – African proverb

Wherever you are in your heart and mind at the outset of a relationship is where you will be at the end. Whatever you bring to the start of the relationship is what you will have to clean up in the end. You cannot begin a relationship in dishonesty and deceit and hope to experience an honest end. If you run into a relationship to get away from another, you will run into another one to get away from this one. If you enter a relationship in fear, anger or grief, you stand a pretty good chance of finding more of the same. If you enter a relationship in sadness, desperation and pain, guess what? You will find it again. If we want to put an end to angry, bitter and ugly separations, we must begin our relationships with the open, loving honesty we say we want. If we do not know who we are and how we feel at any time, it is best that we stay alone.

I will be better at the beginning to avoid anything worse at the end.

28 August

Anything dead coming back hurts.
– Toni Morrison, from *Beloved*

If you keep going in and out of the same relationship, chances are you are going to get hurt. People come together in a relationship to learn. Once you learn your lesson it is time to move on. Take your lesson from the last time and move on to something new. If you insist on drinking from the same used cup, you will eventually get sick. You can do the same old things in just so many ways until you lose track of what you are doing. How many ways can you cry? How many ways can you hurt? How many ways can you convince yourself that you can make this work? When a relationship is over, you must learn to let go. No matter how much you love the other person, or how afraid you are that you will never love again, you cannot squeeze juice from a piece of dry fruit, so don't bother to try.

When it is over, I am on to the next thing.

29 August

Is this love? Is this love? Is this love?
Is this love that I'm feeling?
– Bob Marley

How do you know when you are really in love? First of all, you would not have to ask the question. Love is knowing, it is not a condition or state of mind. When you are loving, you are not doubting, judging or fearing; you are in a state of acceptance. You accept yourself first, for who and what you are, and then the person you love, without question. You do not want to fix him, change him, control him or help him. You want for the person you love exactly what she wants for herself. When you are in love, you feel vulnerable and know that it is okay. You do not hide your feelings, change them to fix what you think the other person wants, and you do not question what you feel. When you are in love, you give, expecting nothing in return, not even love. Love is an inner process between you and yourself that you want to share with someone, everyone. Love is free. If your quest is to own, control, hold on to, protect, or take care of someone, they cannot be free and you are not in love. Love is never wrong, seldom right. It just is.

Love is in the midst of me.

30 August

When self-respect takes its rightful place in the psyche,
you will not allow yourself to be manipulated
by anyone.
– Indira Mahindra

Loving, wanting or being with someone else is absolutely
no reason to abuse, neglect or disrespect yourself. In all
of our relationships, we can only give what we have.
When we have a sense of self, an honest consciousness
of our needs, a clear concept of what we want, we can
respect ourselves. We set the standard of how we want
to be treated, it remains our responsibility to make sure
that anyone and everyone who comes into our lives treats
us as well or better than we treat ourselves. If we are not
honest with ourselves, how can we expect others to be
honest with us? If we are not nurturing and supportive
of ourselves, why would we expect it from anyone else?
If we do not expect and give the best to ourselves, from
where do we think it will come? Our relationships can
only be reflections of the relationships that we
have with ourselves.

*If I love, honour and respect me – you must
do the same.*

31 August

You cannot throw a loved one out of your
heart and mind.
– Betsey Salunek

No matter what they have done to you and said to
you, you cannot stop loving them. No matter how much
they disappoint you, neglect or abuse you, if you think
you love them, you probably do. It does not matter what
others say about them, how others feel about them or
how bad you feel about them; if you love them, admit
it. Do not tell yourself you don't love somebody if you
do. What you might want to do is make a choice about
whether you want this person to be a part of your life.
It is not necessary to stop loving people if you don't like
them. You can choose the type of relationship you want
to have with the people you love. You can love them
from a distance. You can love them and not live with
them. You can love them in the deepest part of your being
and choose to move on. You can figure out why you love
them, if you love them and still choose to move on. You
can love them for who they are and what they are and
stop complaining.

I can choose how I want to love you.

1 *September*

Everything was fine but the beans were salty.
– Mother Jefferson

There are people in your life you can never please no matter what you do. There is always something wrong with you, with the world and with them. Criticism is the way adults cry. When we are in pain, nothing looks or feels good, particularly those close to us. We strike out because we cannot tune into what we are feeling. Criticism is our way of saying something is wrong with us and we see it in you. Do not take it personally when a loved one continuously criticizes. They are never upset for the reason they say they are, and whatever it is, it is not your issue. Do not strike back when you are criticized. Remember, you are with someone who is in pain. Be gentle with them, love them, gently ask them to talk to you about what they are really feeling.

I Am all right with me.

2 September

When one door closes, another one opens.
– African-American folklore

Many people ask, 'Why can't I find a good relationship?' Perhaps it is because they haven't truly ended the last one. We hold on to people in our hearts and minds long after they have gone. We may hold on to anger, hurt and pain. We may be holding ideas of revenge and destruction. We hold on to romantic memories and special times using them as measuring sticks for anyone who comes along. We hold on to our hearts, protecting them from pain, our minds filled with memories and doubts. We believe our dreams are shattered and will never come true. With all of the stuff we hold on to, how can others get into our hearts? We must learn how to close the door on old relationships. We must sort through the rubbish, clear out the garbage and freshen up our hearts and minds to receive a new guest.

I Am closing the door on the past.

3 September

If you believe you are to blame for everything that goes wrong, you will have to stay until you fix it.
– Zora Neale Hurston

Some of us, particularly women of colour, set ourselves up to be martyrs. We are to blame. It is our fault. We just can't seem to do anything right, so we don't. We create mess after mess, crisis after crisis. This allows others to use us as doormats. Smart move! As long as we are to blame, we cannot be held responsible or accountable for what we do not accomplish. We are too busy fixing the mess, figuring out what to do, or if we should do anything at all. As long as we have something or someone to fix, we cannot fix ourselves. We will never fix the fear of our power. We will never fix the fear of our beauty. We cannot fix our pain or confusion or desperate feelings of isolation. We don't have to face our fears or try to fix them; after all, it's our fault we are like this. And as long as we are to blame, we will never have to face the thought that others must share in the responsibility of getting things done.

The only thing I will fix today is me.

4 September

It doesn't matter what road you take, hill you climb,
or path you're on, you will always end up in
the same place, learning.
– Ralph Stevenson

There is nothing more devastating to the human psyche
than what we call a broken heart. He done me wrong!
She put me out! He cheated! She lied! I can't eat! I can't
sleep! I see her face! I hear his voice! Please let him call!
I've got to see her! Wait! Hold it! Hearts don't break!
We love with our heads, not with our hearts. We develop
an idea of what a relationship should be, how our mate
should behave and what we want to feel in the process.
If things do not go the way we planned, our hearts are
broken. There is a secret to this love thing – we must
learn how to love honestly with no preconceived notions.
Loving honestly means being who we are, accepting our
mates for who they are; demanding nothing in return for
our love. Under these conditions, if things do not go well,
it has nothing to do with our hearts; it's our poor choices
that have caught up with us. The only thing we can do
about a broken heart is fix our head.

My heart is unbreakable.

5 September

The only way to have peace in a relationship is to
know how to butter your own bread.
– Ra-Ha

If you are in a relationship that causes you imbalance
and anguish, get out. If you are in a relationship that
does not support you or lowers your energy, leave it
alone. If you are in a relationship where you give more
than you get, where what you give is not respected, where
the security you seek is costing you peace of mind, you've
got nothing else to lose – so leave. We come together in
relationships to grow, not to live in misery. Our relationships should be sustaining, energizing and growth-
supporting. When they are not, our growth is stunted,
our energy is depleted and our personality is distorted.
A solid, loving, supportive relationship is like a shot of
life. It is a source of inspiration, it provides a spark of
motivation to encourage you on to the highest evolution
of your selfhood. If you are in a relationship in which
you are happy sometimes, sad most of the time, struggling to figure out what to do, and how to make it last,
you are out of place.

I know when to quit.

6 September

Make all your relationships an 'eight' or better.
– John Salunek

On a scale where one is low and ten is high, we want to live as close to ten as possible. We want to give and get the best in our relationships. Whether it is a friendship, love affair or business relationship, we must not allow mediocrity to be the standard. When we have no standards our lives become so crowded with people, demands and unrealized expectations that we run the risk of losing ourselves. An 'eight' relationship is one where there is mutual support and respect. We can be who we are and know we are accepted on that basis. There are common goals; even when we disagree on method, we can support the intent. In an 'eight' relationship we give for the joy of giving. We share for mutual growth. We give and get complete honesty. We take what we need and do not fail to give back. An 'eight' relationship is one that we do not work on. It is one we work with and for, striving for better as a mutual benefit. 'One' means you don't have it. 'Six' is just making it. An 'eight' means you are definitely on the way to the top.

There is no reason I must settle for less.

Vulnerability is the gift I give to those I trust
when I trust myself.
– Terry Kellogg and Marvel Harrison

Just because people are nice to us and don't ask anything
in return, does not mean there is something wrong with
them. It is often hard for us to believe people can like us
simply for who we are. Benny, a White man, was willing
to give Frank, a Black man, a kidney. Frank wouldn't
accept it. He had known Benny for three short weeks.
Frank knew very little about Benny. But he knew Benny
must have a hidden agenda. Nobody gives a kidney away
for nothing. Frank confronted Benny with his anger, suspi-
cion and fear. Quietly Benny replied, 'I know you like to
go fishing. I know you are a good father and a loving
husband. I know because that's what you've shown me.
Based on what I've seen, I know you don't deserve to
die.' Frank accepted the kidney. Benny moved to Arizona
and never saw Frank again.

Blessings come in all colours. I get the ones I deserve.

8 September

Love creates an 'us' without destroying the 'me'.
– Leo Buscaglia

Love really is about people coming together to support each other. All the little tricks and games they play to get their needs met are just that, tricks and games. It would be so much simpler if we honoured ourselves and trusted our partners enough to ask for what we need. Instead, we wait for them to figure it out; if they don't, we hold them responsible. What a cruel trick! When we let our partners know up front what we need, we have a greater chance of having the need met. We must know that our needs are important. Whether it's hugs and kisses, foot rubs, reassurance or Hershey syrup and whipped cream, our needs do matter. Once we let our partners know what we need, we must accept their honest answer as to whether or not they can meet those needs. If they cannot, we must then decide if these are the people we want in our lives.

I honour my needs by letting my mate know what they are.

9 September

Loving someone and pleasing someone are
two different things.
– Jerry Jampolski

The mother knew that her teenage son was involved
with some unsavoury people and affairs. She remained
silent when he started wearing expensive clothes. She
turned her head when he flashed the money. She drew
the line when she found the bloody clothes and the gun
in the basement. The next morning she called the police
and had her only son arrested. When the social worker
asked her how she felt about what she had done, she
replied, 'It is a lot easier for me to visit him every week
in prison than it would be for me to take one trip to the
cemetery.' In all of our relationships there comes a time
when we must do what we know is right. If we love
someone, we want the best for them. It may not make
them happy; it probably won't be easy; but loving someone
does not mean allowing them to hurt themselves. It
certainly doesn't mean you must allow them to hurt you.

In loving you I will not lose myself.

10 September

Consider those whom you call your enemies and figure
out what they should call you.
– Dwayne Dyer

You cannot choose sides in a round world. You are
either in it, a part of it, or you are off. When you have
enemies you are a part of the very things you accuse them
of. An enemy opposes your interests or position. An
enemy is hostile, unkind or unfriendly. And what are you
doing while all of this is going on? If you consider them
your enemy how can they approach you to get things
clear? You are in the middle of what stands between you
and your enemy. It is not what they have done or said,
can do or might do; it is you. It is your thoughts, your
judgments, your fear, your condemnation, and if you did
not feel guilty you could not attack those you call your
enemy. You believe the enemy is wrong, not to be trusted,
unworthy of love; you prepare yourself for the defence,
projecting on to the enemy the very things you do yourself. When you have an enemy, look at your own hatred;
understand how the hostility disturbs you and ask yourself, do I really want to attack the very thing I fear?

The only enemies I have are the ones I attack.

11 September

For a love to grow through the tests of everyday living, one must respect that zone of privacy where one retires to relate to the inside instead of the outside.
– Kahlil Gibran

Everybody needs a little time and space where they can go to be alone. What this is called in a relationship is 'the danger zone'. We all need those few little things that we have for ourselves. It could be a thing, place, an activity or something we cannot share. What this can look like in a relationship is 'what is mine is theirs'. Everyone has that special thing that they just love to do. What this feels like in a relationship is 'I'm going out without you.' If you want your relationship to grow and flourish and your loved one to remain living and kind, give them the time, space and opportunity to go and make contact with their own minds.

Today I will let you be with yourself.

12 September

When the law of an eye for an eye operates, all the people will end up blind.
– Bishop Desmond Tutu

You simply cannot pay anyone back for something they did to you. Look for the lesson and move on. If one man treats you badly, rejects you, abandons you, abuses or disrespects you, you cannot hold all men accountable. Look for the lesson and move on. If your ex-wife took your money, lied to you, neglected your children and your home, it does not mean no woman can be trusted. Look for the lesson and move on. If some White people are racists; some Black people thieves; some intellectual people condescending; some uneducated people lazy; some light people uppity; some dark people ignorant; it does not give you the right or the authority to treat all people who look the same or act the same any way you choose, based on your past experiences. Ask yourself, What can I learn from this situation? What can I do this time that I did not do before? If there is nothing, simply move on.

I am doing the best I can right now.

13 September

Every woman is every other woman trying to figure out who she is.
– Nana Korantemaa

Women of colour have been led to believe that they must be everything to everyone. As a result, we do not know how to ask for support when we need or want it. We become angry with others when they are not there for us, but we must realize people cannot, will not and do not know how to help if we do not know how to ask. Take sixty seconds for yourself and ask yourself what you need. If it is assistance with a project, a shoulder to cry on, a special something you need or want for yourself, let other people support you. We make judgments about what people can or will do and we move on our assumptions. We never really know what a person is willing to do or capable of doing until we ask. Nothing is too big or too small to ask for if we need it. When we don't ask for what we need, the need keeps getting bigger.

If I need support today I will ask for it.

14 September

If you can find someone you can really talk to, it can
help you grow in so many ways.
– Stephanie Mills

We all need the time, space and opportunity to vent
our anger, frustration or dissatisfaction with the world.
Unfortunately, those closest to us bear the brunt of our
emotions when we do not release them. If loved ones take
their frustration out on us, we must try not to take it
personally; and never, never tell them they don't really
feel that way. We must learn to honour others' feelings
and support them in expressing how they feel. If they say
things to us that are painful or angry, we must separate
what is truth and what is unreal. Parents must find a way
to express their feelings without taking it out on the children. If we are tired, we should say so. If we are angry,
we should take a walk before we go home. If we allow
ourselves to say what we really feel, when we feel it, and
try listening and not responding, we would probably have
a lot less to fight about. When we express what we feel
the moment we feel it, it won't get mixed in with
everything else.

Today I will talk about what I feel.

15 September

God is my source and my supply, not my husband.
– Bridgette Rouson

There is only one power and one presence operating in our lives. That is the power of the Creative Source. It operates through our consciousness. It draws to us and provides for us in response to how we think. If we are not aware of the power operating in us, through us and for us, we hold our mate responsible to provide the things we want and need. The Source gives us all that we deserve based on our conscious awareness of its presence. If we pressure our mates to give us things, it means we are out of touch. The Source provides our food, clothing and shelter. It provides us with work; it fulfils our needs. The Source may work through things and people, but the Source is the substance of all things. If we have a mate who is not giving, sharing or providing us with the things we think we need, we must ask ourselves, What am I thinking about in terms of where and from whom I get my sustenance?

God, the omnipresent, provides my every need.

16 September

Coming together is a beginning; keeping together is a process; working together is success.
– Henry Ford

Whether in business or personal relationships, what makes working together so difficult is the individual need to be right and to have things our way. As long as we have a position to hold on to we cannot come together or work together. If we are not willing to bend, we will somehow get in the way. We must get clear about what we are doing, why we are doing it and who we are working with. Only with an honest examination of our motives and intent can we surrender to any working or loving process. If we enter any collective agreement for only personal goals and with mental garbage, the stability of the group is jeopardized by our dishonest foundation. If we come together in honesty, work together in clarity, we can stay together with respect and meet any goal successfully.

I respect myself enough to respect the working process.

Most people enjoy the inferiority of their friends, real
friends don't notice it.
– Norman Douglas

Many people of colour believe it is their responsibility
to stay in relationships, communities and situations to
prove they are true blue. Nothing could be further from
the truth! We owe it to our dreams to place ourselves in
an environment that provides and supports the things we
want. We have a right to peace, prosperity and success,
even when it means we leave the "hood'. Does this mean
you think the 'hood is bad? No, it simply means the 'hood
is not where you choose to be. Growth requires that we
move on. Movement does not mean rejection. It means
we want to broaden our scope. To move beyond those
things and people who are familiar to us does not mean
we are leaving them behind. It means we are clearing a
path for them to follow, if they choose to.

New friends are silver, old friends are gold.

18 September

A friend is a person who dislikes the same
people you do.
– Anonymous

Don't hang out with people who are where you don't
want to be. Your friends and the environment reflect what
you really feel about yourself. Winners hang out with
winners. Losers hang out with losers. When you are on
the move, you need people and an environment that
supports and encourages your dream. You won't find that
among people who are helpless and hopeless. You won't
find support for your goals among people who whine and
complain. You must know and believe that there are people
waiting for you in the places you want to be. They will
nurture, support and encourage you to keep moving.
People you know may not always support your growth.
For you to move on means you leave them behind. It also
means that you prove what they claim to be impossible
is definitely possible.

*I surround myself with people and things that are
good for me.*

19 September

When you are kind to someone in trouble, you hope they'll remember and be kind to someone else. And, it'll become like a wildfire.
— Whoopi Goldberg

For some reason which was never fully explained, Robert despised Rhonda. He told anyone who would listen how rotten, no good and downright dislikable she was. He made a campaign of it. He wrote letters. He made telephone calls. When he saw Rhonda, he smiled and said, 'Hello'. Robert died, suddenly, unexpectedly and penniless. There were many things that needed to be done. No one stepped forward to help, except Rhonda. She made the arrangements, spent the money and took care of Robert's affairs as best she could. Robert will never be able to say, 'Thank you'. He's not in a position to say, 'I'm sorry. I was wrong about you.' He will never be able to pay her the money or compensate her for her time. But when Rhonda had a family emergency and needed a car to travel across two states, someone she hardly knew said, 'Here, take my car.'

When I help you, I help me.

20 September

When you are not happy with yourself, you cannot be happy with others.
– Daryl Mitchell

Everyone comes into our life to mirror back to us some part of ourselves we cannot or will not see. They show us the parts we need to work on or let go of. They reveal to us the things we do and the effects they have on ourselves and others. They say to us openly the things we say to ourselves silently. They reveal to us the fears, doubts, weaknesses and character flaws we know we have but refuse to address or acknowledge. We can usually see the faults of others very clearly. We all have people in our lives who anger or annoy us, who rub us the wrong way. They may create confusion or chaos. They may bring pain and disruption. They may reject us, abandon us and create some sort of harm. Before we get busy trying to fix the person or remedy the situation, we should ask ourselves, Why is this person in my life? What am I doing to draw this to myself? How do I do what they do, and how can I release this need? When we cleanse, heal and bring ourselves into balance, everyone in our lives will do the same or disappear.

My relationships are a true reflection of me.

21 September

Your children are not your children.
— Kahlil Gibran

Take time today to remember that your children also have a heavenly Mother and Father who are as concerned about them as you. You are the channel used to bring the child into life, but you are not the only force guiding that life. We can become so preoccupied with what we 'should have' done that we forget how much we are doing. We can be so absorbed with what is 'wrong' with our children that we miss what is right. The fear over their or our failure prohibits our giving them what they need to succeed. Today, focus on the goodness that exists in children! There are things they do well and things they will learn to do better. Know that you cannot fix your children and you cannot plan their lives. What you can do is guide, support, nurture and love them, with all you have, in the best way you can. Once you've done that, know that the heavenly Mother and heavenly Father want as much if not more for them than you do.

I surrender my children to the divine force that moves in, through and for them.

22 September

Some kids do what you say. Some kids do what you say do not do. But all kids do what you do.
– Unknown

A thirteen-year-old was sent to the cleaners. She was told to go straight there; she did. But she did not come straight home. On the trip home from the cleaners, she became involved in an egg fight. More than a half dozen eggs ended up on a $300 suit. She took the suit home, rolled it up, put it in a plastic bag and hid it in the closet. Three days later when she was asked about the suit, she started to cry and produced the bag with the festering suit from the closet. The child is still alive with all of her limbs intact. The parent took a deep breath and reminded herself: There are times when I do not follow instructions; I do not always admit my mistakes and I try to cover them up. When I am put on the spot, I cry. Whenever I am confronted with something I've done wrong, I usually don't lie. If we really want to understand why our children behave the way they do, we must take a long, hard, honest look at ourselves.

When I see my children I see myself.

23 September

It doesn't have to glitter to be gold.
– Arthur Ashe

They always want. They always need. They gave you that first grey hair. They eat too much. They sleep too much. They have a loving relationship with dirt. They break the good dishes. They never wash the glasses clean. They really know how to embarrass you in public. They talk too loud. They walk too slow. They rarely do what you ask, the way you want it done. They go away. They come back with friends and dirty laundry. They worry you. They frighten you. They always want to question you. They love you. They hate you. They always have a great use for your money. They grow up. They get better. They get older. They get worse. Now just think how empty the world would be if we didn't have our children to love.

I really do love my children.

24 September

Children are God in work clothing.

It is hard for our children to tell us what they really feel. They don't want to hurt us. They don't want to be disrespectful. They may not believe what they think and feel is valuable. As parents, it is sometimes hard for us to let them be who they really are – people, with thoughts, feelings and dreams. We want to protect them. We want to give them the best. We must consider whether the things we want for them are the things they want for themselves. What we fear for them they may not fear for themselves. Our children have the right to choose to search, explore and decide, and they have the stamina it takes to fall on their faces and get up again.

*Today I will do more than listen, I will hear
my children.*

25 September

Think wrongly if you please, but in all case think
for yourself.
– Louisa May Alcott

One of the many things that drive parents crazy about
their children is that children like to think for themselves.
Parents do not like that. Most of the time, parents do
not understand why children believe as they do; they may
also feel threatened when the children do not see things
the right way – that is, the parents' way. Parents have
experience; they believe children do not. Parents know
the dangers and traps in life; children seem not to care.
Parents believe that if children are left to their own
devices, they will destroy themselves. Parents need to
realize the difference between discipline and thinking,
disobedience and thinking, disrespect and thinking.
Children are just people living through a smaller body.
They must learn to express themselves, to understand
who they are and grow into who they are through their
own thoughts. Just because your children do not think
as you do doesn't mean they are wrong.

*Ideas are children of the mind. My children
have children.*

26 September

When you say 'I love you,' you are actually saying you have awakened a place in me where I am love.
– John Rogers

Deep within our being is a place of peace, joy and knowing. It is a place called love. We are not taught to live from that place for ourselves. We are taught to shower it on others. We do for others what we will not do for ourselves. We give to others what we think we do not deserve. We turn to others for the very feeling that comes from the self. We are love from the core of our being. It is the energy by which we were born. We breathe love. We see love. We have our being in love. Why can't we learn to love ourselves the same way we love others? If we can live from our being of love, we can't help but attract more of what we are. Love is what we are. When we know that and live through it, we can live 'in love' with ourselves.

I Am love.

27 September

A relationship is placing one's heart and soul in the
hands of another while taking charge of another in
one's soul and heart.
– Kahlil Gibran

When we enter a relationship, we don't often think or
see beyond the physical being. We are attracted to the
body, face or personality. We may like what the person
does or how they do it and want to be a part of that.
We may even experience a pull from within that we can't
actually explain. But how often do we stop to consider
the true depth of the person we are attracted to? There
is a being before us who has a past, present and future.
There is flesh and bones, hurts and scars, feelings, thoughts
and ideals. When we enter the world of another being
we must be willing to be a part of it all. When someone
entrusts their heart to you they are giving you a piece of
their soul. You cannot treat a soul casually. You must
protect, nurture and handle it with care. Our interactions
with one another go far beyond the face, body and hair.
One other thing we must consider when we enter someone's
heart, there is a heart and soul inside of us of which they
will play a part.

*I respect the heart, mind and soul of my friends
and lovers.*

28 September

Experience is a good teacher but she runs up big bills.
— Minna Antrim

If life is about learning and growing, why do we think our relationships are beyond life's classroom? Every relationship – family, friendship, love and marriage – is about growth and development. There are certain skills we need. Certain strengths we must develop. Certain lessons we must learn. Our relationships provide the perfect framework for us. We come together to share, learn and grow. Once we have acquired the skill, imparted the information or learned the lesson, it is time for something else. It is time to move on. That may feel like, 'You don't love me anymore.' What it actually says is, 'You don't have anything else to give me.' If we could move beyond the emotion of it and look for the growth, ending a relationship, moving out of a family or friendship would be a great deal less painful. We want to learn how to be grateful for everything we get in our relations. Somewhere beyond the grief, fear, pain and disappointment is a mighty lesson just waiting to be learned.

Every encounter is an experience of growth.

29 September

I will fear no evil: for thou art with me . . .
– Psalm 23:4

No matter what is happening in your relationships, fear nothing and no one. When you walk with the consciousness of the Creator, there is nothing to fear. Do not fear that people will harm you or leave you. Do not fear people who threaten you. Do not fear obstacles that confront you. Have no fear of harm to your body or possessions, you are walking with the strong arm of the law. Do not fear disapproval. Do not fear criticism. Do not fear judgment. Know that the only energy that has any power in your life is the gift of breath from God. Do not fear places. Do not fear darkness. Do not fear separation or divorce. Do not fear being alone. Do not fear being cast aside. When you walk with the Master, you are in the best company available.

I shall not fear.

Those who don't know how to weep with their whole
heart, don't know how to laugh either.
– Golda Meir

When we lose a loved one to death or end a long-term
relationship, it is perfectly normal to grieve. We must
honour and recognize each stage of the grief and every
emotion we have. There will be shock, denial, anger, confusion, fear, helplessness, numbness, and eventually, acceptance. There will be a point when we do not know what
to do, but we want to do something. At that point we
must understand and accept, there is no death; there is
no end; there is only transformation. Our loved one now
exists in a new time, new place, new reality – and so do
we. The relationship as we knew it has been transformed
from the physical to the spiritual, from marriage to separation, from loveship to friendship; it has not ended; it
has changed. When we allow ourselves to grieve, we release
the negative thoughts and emotions that make it easier
to accept the change. When we do not grieve, we get
stuck. Grief is natural, normal and to be expected. We
owe it to ourselves and the memory of the relationship
to grieve and cleanse our soul.

*I will take the time to grieve and prepare myself for
the change.*

MONEY
AND
ABUNDANCE

1 October

Success Law #107: Put your butt on the line.

If there is something you want to be, have or do in this life, there is only one sure way to find out if you can have it. Put your butt on the line! All the things you want to have; places you want to go; things you want to experience are eagerly awaiting you. It's up to you to go for it. Put your butt on the line! Say what you need to say. Do what you need to do. Ask for what you want, exactly the way you want it. Don't take no for an answer. Put your butt on the line. All you get is what you give, so give it all you've got. Put your butt on the line. If you're satisfied, but still hungry for something out there, somewhere, go for it! Put your butt on the line for what you believe in. Put your butt on the line for what you stand for. Put your butt on the line just to prove to yourself you can do it. Think of it this way, the worst that can happen is that you will end up right where you started, with your butt on the line.

Faith will save my butt when it's on the line.

2 October

Give Thanks!

We have so much in life to be thankful for. We walk, talk, see, hear, think and breathe – usually without effort. Why do we spend so much time dwelling on what we can't do, don't have and what is going wrong? We can instantly recall the negative experiences, people and circumstances without recognizing we have the ability to walk away, get away or make a change. Perhaps we have too many options from which to choose. Or it could be we simply like to complain. Maybe if we spent just a little time saying 'thank you' for what we do have, we won't have so much time to dwell on what we lack. Gratitude, praise and thanksgiving activate the divine laws of abundance. When the universe can see we are conscious of and grateful for what we have, it is activated to shower us with more. Even when it seems that the well is drying up, we can affirm, 'I can hardly wait to see the good that will come out of this.'

My cup runneth over always.

3 October

It is the Father's good pleasure to give you the kingdom
– Luke 12:32

It is time you realized you were born to be successful
and to have wealth. You are not only ensured material
wealth, but abundant wealth of the mind, body and spirit
as well. You have been created in an image of perfection,
with an inborn knowledge of all you need to know. In
the image of the Creator, it is only right for you to have
the abundance of the kingdom. You are a king's kid! Born
into royalty! You should not live in lack or a state of
desperation and need. It is the Creator's will for you to
live richly. It is your duty to claim what is yours. The
riches of the kingdom, the wealth of the world, the infinite supply of the universe is your inheritance. Graciously
accept it right now!

I have inherited an abundance of every good thing.
Thank you.

4 October

In order to cooperate with life you must learn how to
forgive, how to pray, how to give, how to receive, how
to adjust; seeking nothing, giving everything, loving all
people, trusting God, living each moment fully.
– Donald Curtis

You may not have all the money you want. You may
not live in a fancy house or drive expensive cars. Maybe
you haven't found the right man or woman. You may
have a few extra pounds on your thighs. This does not
mean life is over. Actually, it may not have begun. What
we must do is live from the inside so the outside will
become more fun. Give what you have in order to get
what you need. Take what you get with an open heart.
Trust God to bring forth the desires of your heart, forgive
all people for what you believe they have done. Begin
each day with a prayer of gratitude, love all people for
who they are. Possess no things or persons, speak only
of the things that you want. Life is willing to cooperate
with you, but you must know where to start.

*When I cooperate with life, the forces of life cooperate
with me.*

5 October

If you go to God with a thimble, you can only bring
back a thimbleful.
– Randolph Wilkerson

Ann spent six and a half months living in a basement
with rats and mice. Every day she prayed for a safe place
to sleep. Her prayers were finally answered. A friend
offered her the living room sofa. After two weeks of living
out of shopping bags, she started praying again. 'Please!
All I want is a room with a bed.' Three months later her
daily prayer was heard. She found a six-by-nine-foot
room with enough space for her body, a bed, and four
milk carts to hold her clothes. Why didn't Ann ask for
a three-bedroom house with a basement, backyard and
garage? Because like most of us, Ann's tendency was to
limit God. For some reason we get stuck in our immediate need and we think God is stuck there too. We
believe that the one who created the earth, sun, stars,
mountains, rivers, oceans and trees has nothing left to
give. How long will it take us to realize we have an unlimited account with the universal bank? Our prayers make
the withdrawals. Our faith is the deposit.

I will receive exactly what I ask for.

6 October

There are four rungs on the ladder of success: Plan
Purposefully, Prepare Prayerfully, Proceed Positively,
Pursue Persistently.
– African-American folklore

In everything you do, have a purpose. Make sure the
quality of your intent is one of truth, honour and love.
Prepare to pursue your purpose with prayer. Ask for guidance, protection and direction. Ask that closed doors be
opened and that the purpose of those that remain closed
be revealed. Give thanks for your answered prayers by
proceeding without any doubt. Keep your purpose in mind,
trust the guidance you receive, have faith in your ability
to succeed and accept all that comes your way. If your
purpose is clear, your prayers backed by faith, your outlook
sure and positive, never, never look back. You may meet
forks and turns in the road, but your obstacles shall all
be removed.

*I am planning with purpose, preparing with prayer,
proceeding positively in persistent pursuit of my goal.*

Could it be, He saved the best for last?
– African-American spiritual

Very often we become angry, anxious or fearful when the things we want do not seem to be coming our way. We watch others. We judge whether they have worked hard enough. We criticize them in support of our determination, that they don't deserve to get or have what they want. We doubt ourselves, our ability and worthiness. We blame people and conditions, believing they can stand in our way. The only thing that stands in our way is doubt, fear, criticism and judgment of ourselves and others. As long as we believe someone or something other than ourselves can deny or delay our good, we are not ready to have it. The all-giving, all-knowing Creator is the source of all supply, and He wants you to be ready. When you are strong in heart and mind, when you honestly want for others the good you seek for yourself, you will be well-equipped to have the very best you desire.

I Am preparing myself for the highest and the best.

8 October

What you see, is what you get.
— Flip Wilson

When we are in a dark room, we quickly realize it is easier to see with the lights on. If we've ever been imprisoned, oppressed, in bondage to anyone or anything, we develop a yearning desire for freedom. We learn to appreciate good health when we are sick. We respect wealth when we are in poverty. It seems quite natural to define one condition by what appears to be its opposite. Freedom and oppression, illness and good health, poverty and wealth, happiness and sorrow, peace and confusion, faith and fear, strength and weakness, male and female – these are not opposing powers. They are the results of how the one power of life is used. The ancestors knew that everything comes from one source. They knew this source had the only power and everything else was a minor challenge. When we stay centred on the source, the power, we see that there are no opposites. Only light coming out of darkness to help us see where we want to go.

There is only one Power, one Source operating in my life.

Possession of material riches without inner peace is like
dying of thirst while bathing in the river.
– Paramhansa Yogananda

Howard Hughes is a classic example of what it is like
to gain wealth and lose your soul. He and many others
like him should reinforce the idea that money cannot buy
happiness, peace or health. This seems to be a contra-
diction. On the one hand you need money to get the
things that will make you peaceful, happy and healthy.
On the other hand the pursuit of money can bankrupt
your mind, body and spirit. What is a person to do? Do
Not Chase Money! Do what you do, using your talents
and abilities because it makes you happy. Do Not Do
Things for Money Only! In everything you do, have a
purpose, principle or ideal that you hold dear and will
not compromise if the price is right. Use Things to Help
People; Do Not Use People to Get Things! If what you
want or what you are doing is not the highest and the
best for everyone involved, leave it alone.

Prosperous, prospering peace is my money.

10 October

Your failures in life come from not realizing your
nearness to success when you give up.
– Yoruba proverb

In setting goals, we sometimes box ourselves into time
limits. Limits are fine when we have everything we need
within our control. No matter who we are and what we
want, we must always surrender the element of time to
the divine timekeeper. When we are not conscious of this
element, we may throw our hands up in despair and walk
away a moment before the breakthrough. Our ideas and
goals are the children of our minds. We nurture them
with our thoughts and actions. Like a foetus in the womb,
they develop in just the right way, at the right time.
Eventually, labour will start. It is painful and sometimes
long, but eventually the child comes into life.

Time is on my side.

11 October

You don't own the future you don't own the past.
Today is all you have.
– Les Brown

It is never a good idea to bank on what we may have tomorrow. It makes even less sense to dwell on what we had yesterday. The only thing that really matters is what we can do right now. One of the greatest stress inducers in our lives is tomorrow, for it is the unknown. We worry if 'it' will happen, if 'it' would happen, what if 'it' does happen. Then we spend time planning for what may never come. We do that because we think we know the past. We remember it so well, particularly the pain, the dark days, the unpleasantness we've seen. We spend our present time and energy protecting the future from the past. We fail to realize one is over and the other has yet to come. What we know is now and we have complete control over it – now. Nothing can be promised, nor can we own what is no longer. If we do our best in this moment, we have no time to worry about what may come or has gone.

I Am living in this moment.

12 October

What you give you get, ten times over.
– Yoruba proverb

We have been trained and conditioned to give gifts on specific occasions. Occasionally we give gifts to those who have a special meaning to us. Unfortunately, this kind of giving is more for ourselves than for the person receiving the gift. Usually, we tell ourselves, 'I don't have anything to give.' We have been miseducated about gift-giving. We believe gifts must always bear a price tag or be given for a particular reason. It is this kind of thinking that causes a drought in our giving supply. The real joy in giving comes when we give what we have spontaneously, with no reason other than for the joy of giving. It is this kind of giving that opens the door for us to receive. When we give for the sake of giving, rather than out of duty, we will begin to understand. We can give our time, our energy, our thoughts. We can give a book when we've finished it, something we can no longer wear or use, pay the toll for the car behind us, or give someone we don't know a compliment. We actually have a great deal to give in many ways.

*I give joyously from my heart just for the
sake of giving.*

13 October

Ask for what you want.
– African-American folklore

There is absolutely no reason to ever settle for less than the best. The only reason you get less is because you don't ask for exactly what you want. Sometimes you may think you don't deserve more than you have. At other times we think we want too much. You may believe that if you get what you want, you will lose something else or something bad will happen to take what you already have. It's as if a waiter spirit is waiting and asking, 'How would you like it?' Let your mind scan life's menu, make a decision knowing whatever you want is available. Ask for what you want, the way you want it. From that moment on, believe it is yours.

*I make my requests from life clear, specific
and plentiful.*

14 October

Stop doing. Start being.

Have you ever noticed that the more you try to do, the less you get done? The reason is that doing requires evaluation and activity on the physical level. The physical part of us is limited by perception and personality. Our perceptions tell us what we can do, can't do, will do, won't do and what others will think, do and say about our 'doing'. Doing is an intellectual exercise. The more we value our intellect, the more we think we must do. The key is to stop doing and start being. We must accept our goodness right where we are and stop thinking of it as something we must wait to get. Whatever it is you want to be is waiting for you. You can be healthy, organized, loved, prosperous, fulfilled and free without 'doing' anything. It begins with a single thought and a simple statement . . .

I AM.

15 October

No matter what you can see, there is always more.
— Dennis Kimbro

Take a ring of keys, place them in front of you. What do you see? Keys, right? Wrong. What is a key? What does it represent? A way in, a way out. A home. A car. Employment. Businesses making keys, providing shelter and protection for families. A steel mill, workers burning ore, machines creating heat, extracting metal used for keys. Migrant workers in mines, minimal wages providing food, small villages with dusty roads, ragged huts that don't need keys. Steel-industry inheritance, caviar, a Jaguar; mansions with many doors, many locks that need many keys. Hot steel being shaped, not enough air, black lung disease. Fire extracting metal, interstate travel, truckers moving metal, making machines, to make keys. The key is never what you see. There is always more.

I Am not fooled by appearances, the best is yet to come.

It is the fool whose own tomatoes are sold to him.
– Akan proverb

People of colour are great and creative producers. Yet they are even more consistent consumers. We have given so much to the world and for some strange reason, we keep buying it back. We cannot complain about what we lose if we allow it to be taken. We cannot complain about what others do to us if we are not doing for ourselves. If we as a people are ever to stand, we must give credit to one another for the things we create. We must take every necessary precaution to safeguard what is ours. Buy in our own communities first. Educate our children well. Protect the women and elders at all costs. Give to our own expecting nothing in return. Above all, do not allow the love of money to supersede our pride for our people.

I recognize the value and value all that I have.

Sooner or later it catches up with you.
– African-American folklore

The universe is so intelligent, it never asks us how or why. Our thoughts, words and deeds are quietly recorded and we are always paid our due. There are times when we can't figure out how we got to where we are, or why we go through what we do. We just can't seem to figure it out, but the universe knows. There is an invisible bank of law and order into which we all deposit. At just the right time, in just the right way, we are given an account. We must be careful of what we ask for because we will always get it. What we do unto others, shall be done unto us. What we hold in our hearts stays with us. That on which we focus our thoughts will grow. Get the idea?

I thank the universe for revealing what I am thinking about and feeling.

18 October

What makes you think the world owes you something?
– Gwendolyn Brooks

So many people go through life believing they are being cheated or that the world owes them something. This world owes us nothing except the opportunity to express our highest self. The world does not owe us a house. We are not owed a car. We are not owed money, furs or diamonds because the opportunity to have is ours at birth. The Creator has wisely provided us with the most important things in life – the air to breathe, the sun to warm and nurture, the abundant beauty of nature and the opportunity to choose. Divine guidance and inspiration are available to all whenever they are needed. By believing that certain things are only given to certain people, we get stuck without realizing all is available to all. We must ask those who believe they are owed something from whom do they think it will come?

All that I am owed comes to me by choice.

19 October

You get what you expect.
– Alvin Ailey

We often say we want many things while deep inside we doubt it will come to us. The universe does not give us what we say we want; it gives us what we expect to get. You cannot fool Mother Nature. She gives birth to your deepest thoughts and the principle is this: Everything happens twice – first on the inside, then on the outside. We must literally create the energy of what we want within ourselves before we can have it in the physical world. How does it feel to be wealthy? In love? In perfect health? Totally free to do anything we choose? We must let the feeling well up inside and live as though the very thing we want is the thing we have. We must feel ourselves being and enjoying the very best life has to offer. We must think about it, talk about it and expect it every moment. We must impregnate our total being with the expectation of what we want. As the feeling grows, the day will come when we give birth to exactly what we want.

I expect all the best right here and now.

20 October

He'll give you as far as you can see.
— First Church of Deliverance

We have the ability, right and power to create whatever we want in our lives. All we have to do is see it. We can choose to see the unlimited possibilities, rich opportunities and uncharted waters. We can choose to see that doing what we want with ease, having what we want with joy and being where we want can be used for projection and perception. When we use our eyes to project what we want into the world, we send forth the creative power of the soul's force. When we use positive perception to interpret what we see, we avoid falling prey to doom and gloom. If we can look beyond today, its challenges and obstacles, we can create a better tomorrow. If we can see, it must come to be. That is the law.

I Am willing to see my good.

21 October

When you focus on the problem, the problem
gets bigger.

The mind is such an incredible power that it literally
expands whatever it touches. When we are faced with a
challenge, obstacle or problem, our tendency is to nurture
it. We talk about it. We describe it vividly. We monitor
its progress day by day, imagining how much it is growing
and how its effects are devastating every aspect of our
lives. What we are actually doing is giving the problem
more value than it's worth. When confronted with a difficulty, we must immediately shift our attention from the
problem to the solution. We can think, speak and bring
the best possible outcome into existence by focusing on
where we are going, not on where we think we are.

My positive, faithful attitude quickly brings my good.

Stretch your hands as far as they reach, grab all
you can grab.
– Yoruba proverb

You look inside a packed moving van, but you cannot find a place for the last box. You take a chance, climb over all the other boxes and find there is just enough room at the top. If there were only room for one at the top, we would have only one brand of chocolate chip cookies, one brand of tea and only one kind of potato chips. We must never allow ourselves to be guided or stopped by what anyone else is doing. We must never allow ourselves to think we can only go so far because others are already there. When we reach up, stand on our toes, stretch our hands out and grab as much as we can hold. If we want to keep our hands full and the good-ness flowing to us, we must never, ever forget to say 'thank you' for every little thing.

I Am grateful there is always room for me.

Money is in abundance, where are you?
– Reverend Ike

Do you know that you are as rich as any individual walking the earth? Do you know that you have the keys to unlock unlimited inexhaustible wealth? Do you know gold, silver and piles of warm, loving money is yours, right now? If you answered no to any of these questions, you have not developed a prosperity consciousness. Prosperity is a state of mind. It goes beyond money or the things money can buy. It requires you to release the anger, hurt and disappointment of yesterday in order to embrace the goodness in your life today, without fear of the uncertainties of tomorrow. Prosperity is freedom, peace, good health, simplicity and love. Prosperity is knowing who you are, loving it and doing what you love. When you think prosperity and act prosperously you will contract bountiful wealth.

My prosperity begins as a state of mind.

If you want to be a millionaire, you have to
think like one.
– Dr Johnnie Coleman

Most people want to be rich. They spend so much time wishing the money would come that they cannot figure out how to bring it to themselves. The rich-wishing people don't seem to realize that if you want to be rich you have to think richly. People who think richly do not believe in lack. People who think richly know nothing costs too much. People who think richly believe they are worthy of the best – that is why they always get it. People who think richly don't always have money. What they have is a rich consciousness. Unless we have a consciousness that mirrors what we want, we cannot draw it to us. Unless we believe we deserve the things we want, our thoughts will push them away. We must not limit ourselves to what we think we can have. We must allow ourselves to think we can have it all. Millionaires are born in the consciousness. If you are living in lack, what are you thinking?

I Am making millions in my mind.

25 October

Decide that you want it more than you are afraid of it.
– Bill Cosby

So many times in life we allow fear to stop us in our tracks; the sad thing is we don't always recognize we are afraid. We find excuses and rationalizations. We create responsibilities, true and false, we must tend to before we can move forward. We create challenges and obstacles so real in our minds that they manifest in our lives. Behind it all is fear. Fear we are not good enough. Fear we won't be liked. Fear that if we do it once, someone will ask us to do it again and we won't be able to. What are our excuses? Who or what is stopping us? How many times do we talk ourselves out of what we say we really want? What are we afraid of?

I put desire above fear every day.

26 October

Pray for a continuous flow in the now, rather than a
contingent flow in the need.
– BarbaraO

Need represents lack. It says we are in some way
deprived, unable to provide for the self. Need feels
desperate and often we get stuck in that desperation. We
don't always realize that God provides for our needs
without any effort on our part. We need food, clothing
and shelter, of which there is an abundance. The issue is,
Do we want what is available? Usually not; so we think
we need more. We think we need a new coat, a VCR, a
late-model car. We want these things, and that is fine.
Want places us in the driver's seat. It says we are open,
ready and willing to receive. Want says we have a dream,
a goal or an idea we desire to manifest in our lives. Need
makes us fearful. Want helps us to become creative and
responsible. When we strive only to meet our needs, we
are never satisfied. When we strive to satisfy our wants,
we become alive.

All that I need comes to me easily. I want the best.

27 October

Life doesn't have to be a strain or a struggle.
– Marion Anderson

Sometimes we make life very difficult for ourselves. We have a great ability to create our own stress. We may refuse to see the good in anything or anyone. We sometimes refuse to count our blessings and complain about lack. We will criticize, judge or blame others because we forget when our choices were not wise. What we don't seem to realize is that when we voice words of struggle and strife we draw more of it into our experience. We create our own well-being according to the way we conduct our mind, mouth and heart. When we expect the best, we get it. When we speak of good, we see it. When we cleanse our hearts of fear, anger and strife, we place ourselves on a higher vibration. If we choose to struggle with the issues of life, they will be very willing to fight us.

I Am going to create a great day.

Don't show an indifference to money.
– Reverend Ike

How many times have you passed a penny on the street without bending down to pick it up? Don't you think a penny is money? Penny has a mother, her name is dime. Dime has a father; his name is dollar. Dollar has many relatives in all different sizes. Dimes and dollars are very peculiar about how you treat penny. A person with a million dollars who loses a penny is no longer a millionaire. A person who needs a penny to buy a loaf of bread may not eat. We pick and choose the kind of money we want. We may not realize money has a vibration, and if we treat money right it will draw like unto it. The next time you find a penny, do not be indifferent; pick it up, value it, take it home and realize you now have in your possession a close relative of the dollar.

My money vibrates, drawing like unto like.

29 October

You can't have what you want until you want
what you have.
– Horace Harris

The universe is extremely responsive to our strongest thoughts and emotions. The forces of life are eager to bring us the very things we give force to. When we are unhappy, dissatisfied or unfulfilled, we give a great deal of energy to the condition we are in. We must realize that complaining about where we are or what we have is the best way to ensure things stay exactly as they are. We will not attract better or do more until we respect and appreciate what we have now. When our needs and wants seemingly go unmet, we should remember what we do not need. If we consider that we have ended up with the shortest end of the stick, we should consider those who have no stick at all. The only way to prove ourselves to the universal forces is to be grateful and appreciative of what we have now. When we are grateful for the minor, the powers that be carry us over to the grand.

I Am grateful for now.

If you do not re-verse your ways of thinking, speaking and doing, you will remain on the wheel of no motion.
– Ralpha

There are universal laws that govern our ability to multiply and have supply. The law of forgiveness, when put into action, infuses the mind with natural, healthy ideas that take away the darkness and bring in the light. The law of obedience governs our movements, requiring that we act in order and harmony. The law of sacrifice says we must give in order to receive. For everything we give must be returned, as a sacrifice never goes unnoticed. The law of increase requires that we give praise and thanks for all that we have. The law of receiving gives us exactly what we expect. The law of attraction brings to us without delay the desires and thoughts we hold in our minds. The law of supply provides all of our needs and desires, based on our belief of its existence. When our efforts do not multiply, when our supply is not sufficient, it is quite possible that we are breaking the law.

I live within the boundaries of the law.

31 October

When 'I' am here, God is not. When God is here, 'I'
am not.
　　　　– Bawa Muhaiyaddeen

If God is the source of life, shouldn't we be able to find the essence of the source in our lives? Yet when we examine our lives, in what part do we find God? What part is the 'I'? God is love, peace, abundance, power, strength, mercy, truth, balance and joy. For many of us, life is lack, limitation, strife, stress, chaos, confusion, oppression and hate. Your race, my race; their goals, our goals; your religion, my religion have replaced the sense of oneness known as God. Did God create this mess? No, 'I' did. The small part of 'I' that wants control and power. The 'I' that is fear, arrogance, anger and pride. The 'I' that holds on to pain because 'I don't know what to do.' The 'I' that wants it my way because 'I can take care of myself.' The 'I' that can't figure out which part God is and which part 'I' am because 'I' have forgotten that all that God is I Am. If only 'I' would let God do His part, we would be fine.

God, how can I serve you today?

1 November

Inhale the future, exhale the past; inhale the good,
exhale the goop!
– BarbaraO

Inhale. Exhale. Inhale. Exhale. What a wonderful gift
of life. Inhale. Exhale. Inhale. Exhale. The beginning and
the end. Inhale peace, exhale confusion – it is just that
simple. Inhale faith, exhale worry – that is all you have
to do. Inhale order, exhale confusion – get into the flow
of life. Inhale love, exhale anger – feel the warmth flow
through your being. Inhale strength, exhale fear – now
put your mind to rest. Inhale silence, exhale chatter – feel
your body settle. Inhale freedom, exhale restriction – let
your mind follow the dream. Inhale victory, exhale defeat
– prepare yourself for the best. Inhale acceptance, exhale
judgment – feel your self opening. Inhale confidence, exhale
doubt – enjoy the rhythm of who you are. Inhale. Exhale.
Inhale. Exhale. Breath is the gift of grace. As long as we
have it, we have the divine opportunity to go it again.

I accept the gift of breath as a gift of life.

2 November

If we never faced adversity, our well-being would not be as sweet.
– Terry Kellogg

Is there a persistent problem plaguing you? Does it seem to just loom over your head waiting to swoop down and devour you? Is it a money problem? A relationship? A choice or decision you can't seem to make? Do you feel as if you have been backed into a corner with no way out? Good! That is exactly where you need to be! Now take your mind off the problem and laugh. That's right, laugh. Stare adversity in the face. Stop trying to figure out what to do. You are probably thinking this is your punishment for something you did in the past. Or maybe you think it's some more of your 'bad luck'. Well, just throw those thoughts out of your brain and replace them with 'I know there is a power for good in the universe and I call that power forth right now to perfect every condition in my life.' But of course this sounds too easy, too good to be true. You want it to be hard, right? Well, here's something hard for you to work on, 'Be ye transformed by the renewal of your mind!'

Just for today I will laugh in the face of adversity.

3 November

The finger of God never points where the hand of God
isn't somehow making a way.
– Rev Alvin Kibble

When you have a deep burning desire to do a thing,
do it! 'De' meaning 'of', 'sire' meaning Father, is the very
thing God wants for you. The urging is from the soul
and is the only fuel you need. It is a blessing. It lets you
know that you have been chosen for a special task. The
Creator knows you can and wants you to do or have
whatever it is. It cannot be too difficult! It is not beyond
your reach! It is connected to your soul! That's where all
the power is! Trust those urgings. They are the best
friends you could have. Learn to move beyond what
appears to be the essence of what you are. Is it a good
thing? Will you and others benefit? If so, go for it! Don't
let others talk you out of your desire. It is not for them
to see or know. They cannot feel it the way you do, don't
expect them to. Nurture your desire in thought, word
and deed; never doubt it will become your reality. If you
do your part, the Father will do His part and guide you
to the wellspring of your desire come true.

*I can't do it. I Am the conduit through which it will
be done.*

4 November

God would not give us the ability and opportunity to be successful and then condemn us to mediocrity.
— Debra Anderson

Everything in the world was, at one time, just an idea in someone's mind. The chair you are sitting on. The clothes you are wearing. The car you drive. The multimedia instruments that bring information to us. They were all ideas that someone took the time, had the faith and made the commitment to bring forth. How many good, no, great ideas have you had lately? Do you have ideas about things you would like to do? Ideas about the quality of your life? How to make life better for someone else? Why then are you not acting on those ideas? Ideas are all we have. That's what we get from the One on high. We already have the ability, skill and access to information. What the Creator does is generate ideas. Many people get the same idea at the same time. Some of us act, others don't. The next time you are wondering what you are supposed to do in life, remember all the idea blessings you let go.

Go ahead, God, talk. I'm listening.

5 November

If your brain can move your body with a split second command thought, imagine what it can do with concentrated and directed thought.
– Dr Therman Evans

Everyone wants to know the secret of a long, happy, prosperous and successful life. It's no secret. It's an attitude. An energy. A formula. Want to know it? Here it is: (1) Do all things in peace; (2) Achieve personal unity of heart and mind; (3) Learn truth; (4) Maintain your body; (5) Correct character imperfections; (6) Be free from fear; (7) Live in harmony with all people; (8) Eliminate worry; (9) Be poised; (10) Give love; (11) Admire, respect and trust yourself; (12) Know God; (13) Express God; (14) Know what works for you; (15) Help others; (16) Make, have and keep good friends; (17) Solve your own problems; (18) Find your proper place; (19) Have a true marriage; (20) Discover and use your personal talents; (21) Acquire knowledge; (22) Share what you learn with others; (23) Relax; (24) Sleep well; (25) Awake with enthusiasm; (26) Stop unwanted habits; (27) Think positively; (28) Always give thanks for everything you have!

I will prosper because I give thanks.

6 November

The moment you move out of the way, you make room for the miracle to take place.
– Dr Barbara King

You will never accrue the wealth, experience the success, do the things you really want to do as long as you worry about it. Chances are you are thinking in terms of what you do not have and cannot do. Your good cannot get to you if your mind is filled with lack. You have no room for blessings if your words are laced with limitations. You will not notice or be open to new experiences if you are stuck in the old ones. What you want may be totally new to you. It may be way beyond your highest expectations. How can it get to you if you keep getting in the way? It's time for you to move, realizing that the thing you are seeking is also seeking you. If not, you wouldn't want it. That is the law of compensation, what you give out will be returned to you. Get rid of your bad thoughts, inferior attitudes and limited behaviours and good will be attracted to you. It's not easy. It's not magic. But it works, miraculously.

I will not stand in the way of my own good.

Work is love made visible. Keep working with love.
— Anonymous

Have you ever watched people who love what they do? They work with a smile on their faces or a song in their hearts. They move with grace and ease. They attend carefully and lovingly to every little detail. They never tire of what they do. They do it willingly, joyously for themselves, for you and for anyone else who shows the slightest bit of interest. They talk about what they do, they read about it, staying up on the latest trends, teaching it or some part of it to newcomers and converts. When you love your work, it's like a love affair. You do it with a passion. The lust for it rises up from within your soul and makes you giddy. You want to do it all the time, in as many ways as possible. Wherever you go, whomever you're with, you want to do what you love because it feels so good.

I love what I do and I do it with a passion.

8 November

Your wealth can be stolen, but the precious riches
buried deep in your soul cannot.
– Minnie Riperton

Do you like money? Wouldn't you like to have some?
Or even better, wouldn't you like to have a lot of money?
Do you find yourself chasing it? Doing things to get
money or wondering how much money you will get for
doing things? Do you see things you want and remember
you don't have money? Do you think about the places
you would go if you had money? The longer you think
about money, the more you chase money, the longer you
will do without it. Money is very much like a hard-to-
get lover. It eludes you. It teases and tempts you. It gets
your blood flowing and then it runs away. Money will
drive you crazy. The more you want it, the less you will
have of it. It will fight your advances. It will turn on you.
It will leave you high and dry. The best thing you can do
to money is ignore it. Don't chase it. Don't lust after it.
Don't let it invade your mind. Do what you do without
giving any thoughts to money and when you least expect
it, money will fall right into your lap.

*Unexpected doors are open. Unexpected channels
are free.*

9 November

If you keep your pockets full of coins, you will always have small change.
— Yoruba proverb

If you expect to get something for nothing, or if you feel good when you get something without paying for it, you are violating the law of abundance. The law of abundance says you must pay for what you get. You cannot benefit from the mistake or loss of another. If you do, you will someday be forced to pay. Are you a bargain hunter? If so, you are violating the law of vibration. Cheap thoughts bring cheap returns. When you place yourself in low vibration, you draw things that vibrate on the low level. Do you begrudgingly spend money? Do you hate to pay your bills? If so, you are violating the law of correspondence. What you withhold from the universe will be withheld from you. If you give begrudgingly, people will begrudgingly give to you. It is not what you do not have that makes or keeps you poor. It is what you do with what you have that opens the door to more. Pay your way or at least offer to pay. Expect the best and give it to yourself. Release your money happily, being grateful that you have it to give.

The laws are on my side. I am blessed.

Imagine what a harmonious world it could be if every
single person, both young and old, shared a little of
what he is good at doing.
– Quincy Jones

We all come into this life with talents, gifts or abilities
which, if we put them to use, they would be profitable
to us and useful to the world. Yet, we allow ourselves to
be told and we tell ourselves that we're not good enough
or that no one is interested in what we can do. Many of
us spend the greater portion of our lives seeking author-
ization or recognition, never developing or using the
goodness of the things we do naturally. If we would trust
life and ourselves a little more, we would do what comes
naturally, what we are good at, giving it all that we've
got. If we would stop looking for fame and fortune we
might find we are sitting on a goldmine of ideas and abilities. If we would stop blaming others and being ashamed
of ourselves, there would be no way we could expect or
accept anything less than the best from ourselves and for
ourselves. If we would stop chasing castles in the sky and
do what we can do, where we are, the world would probably appreciate it and reward us greatly.

I am willing to give the world who I Am naturally.

11 November

I could do better if I wanted to!
– Dr Oscar Lane

There is a natural, universal force called the law of correspondence. According to this law, you will attract to you that which you are. The law is activated by your dominant thought patterns. The purpose of this law is to show where you are in your consciousness and to give you the opportunity to lift yourself to where you want to be. You can do any good thing you want to do with the right adjustment of your thoughts and actions. If you want prosperity and success, you must change your thoughts to reflect the things you want. Many people live and die never experiencing anything greater than what is handed down to them. If you are born amidst lack, failure, struggle and limitation, you do not have to stay there. Do not claim inherited limitations. The law of correspondence can and will move you to the heights of your consciousness. You cannot attract better, however, until you can better lift your thoughts. Lift your expectations. Lift yourself. Train yourself to mentally look for the good things you want and the good will respond.

I see myself with all the best. I see myself with it now.

12 November

When people say it's not the money it's the principle,
it's the money.
– Stuart Wilde

People of colour don't like to talk about money; we do not want others to know how much we have. We are ashamed to admit when we don't have any. We can talk all day about politics, sex or religion, but when it comes to money, the room gets very still. We don't like to charge money for the things we do. We don't like to collect money for the things we've done. We don't like to give money. We get very nervous when the money we expect does not come when we expect it. Where did we get the notion that there is something wrong with money? Is it our childhood trauma? Is it what we think money can do? Is it our experience of not having much? Is it a fear that having money will somehow cause us harm? Perhaps somewhere deep in our consciousness we realize that money demands respect. And that is something we are not quite ready to do.

I can freely and openly talk about money without shame or fear or guilt.

13 November

The abundance you desire to experience must first be
an experience in your mind.
– Ernest Holmes

Open your mind, heart and soul to accept that it is the
Creator's will for you to have plenty. How else can the
creative force glorify itself? If you are expressing lack,
how can you express faith and love? Today, continuously
affirm, 'My income exceeds my outgo.' As you affirm,
know that you are receiving a substantial increase in your
income. It will exceed your greatest expectations. It will
exceed all of your financial commitments. You have plenty
to spare. New doors of opportunity are opening to you.
New ideas are pouring forth. As you open your mind to
accept your glorious new good, you find new ways to
express faith and love. Abundance may be a new experience for you, but if you open your mind, you will come
to understand that the creative source finds great pleasure
in giving you plenty.

I Am an abundant being experiencing the gift of plenty.

If you think poor, you are poor.
– Wally Amos

It is said that the mind is a terrible thing to waste. Thoughts of poverty and lack are a waste of the valuable power of the mind. In order to experience wealth, success and well-being, it is necessary to train the mind to think positively. Positive thinking is more than a cliché. It is an attitude that embraces the wealth of the human experience. The mind is a tool that can turn a negative into a positive with a stream of progressive thoughts. Many of us have no idea about the true wealth of the universe. We are so accustomed to lack that we see everything as not enough. It is only through the mind, the power of thought, the transformation of perceptions that we will move from being poor to a state of conscious wealth. Take a penny and commit to collecting 999,999 more. In the end you'll have more than a bunch of pennies. You'll have the beginning of a fortune.

Today I will think abundance, prosperity and wealth into my experience.

15 November

Guilt, shame and money go hand in hand.

Parents of all races have berated and belittled themselves over what they could not do for their children because they didn't have the money. Children have the warm, loving, nurturing relations with their parents in exchange for shame over what their parents couldn't afford. There is something wrong with a nation that places monetary value above the greatest gift of life – love. There is something wrong with the people of a nation who continue to measure self-worth in terms of net worth. It is true that money can make life a little easier, more comfortable and perhaps exciting. Money, however, does not make life. Love, supportive parents, good health and a well-ordered mind are absolutely free. And they are nothing to be guilty about or ashamed of.

Money cannot make me and will not break me.

16 November

Have you had it? Owing? Borrowing? Can't have it?
Can't buy it?
— Les Brown

Something is wrong when, as children, we are kept in
the dark about money. So often, because our parents view
money as an issue to struggle with, they do not talk to
us about it. As children, many of us were not allowed to
question anything, so we never asked about financial issues.
To some, money was used as a punishment or reward.
This moulded and shaped our views about it. In other
cases, our parents used money as a weapon against each
other or against us. How can we expect to be financially
responsible if we never received positive instructions about
money? Well, now it's up to us. We owe it to ourselves,
our self-esteem and our future to get the right idea about
money. Many of us feel ashamed, guilty or uncomfortable when we ask questions about money. What we need
to accept and realize is that those who ask questions do
not lose their way.

Money is nothing to be afraid of.

17 November

When you get the bills in the mail, it's like you
just can't breathe.
– Michael Phillips, from *The Seven Laws of Money*

When you are experiencing financial chaos, your
primary goal is to be free of debt. This requires discipline
and structure. You may rebel against the notion of discipline because it feels as if you are being punished. But
you must realize that you are punishing yourself. When
you live beyond your means, if you spend without a budget,
if you live without a plan you are punishing yourself and
your creditors. When you are in debt, spending money
without discipline means you are spending other people's
money. You are withholding from the flow. You are
blocking your abundance. If lack of discipline put you in
debt, only discipline will get you out. As hard as it may
be, as unfair as it may seem, your money is not your
money when you are in debt. Give what you have to
those whom you owe if you want your money to be
rightfully yours.

When I am patiently disciplined my progress is assured.

18 November

Never settle for the crumbs of life.
– Og Mandino

If you are not happy with where you are in life, you don't have to stay there. Don't you deserve better? Don't you want better for yourself and your future? Well, you are the only one who can make it happen. Sure, you've had some pretty rough times, even some pretty devastating ones. There is nothing which says that must be the norm. There are some very difficult challenges and negative attitudes you will confront, but you are equipped to handle it all. There may be some pretty stupid ideas about who you are, what you can do and how far you can go. So what! People also said the world was flat and the moon was made of cheese! The only thing that really matters is what you think, what you believe and what you want. If you have the desire and the will, you will be shown the way.

Greater is that within me than the problem
in the world.

19 November

Lack of money is the root of all evil.
– Reverend Ike

Each day, around the country, thousands of people become ill from the stress of not having money. Once they become ill, they are subject to inadequate health care because they don't have money. Each day, hundreds of creative, talented people sit wasting away because they don't have money. Don't have money to do what? To think? To take care of themselves? To create? We are conditioned to believe that if we don't have money, we have nothing. That is an evil thought. It's evil that robs us of our faith in ourselves and in the process of life. The darkness of it dims the light of human potential. We abandon our dreams, live below our own standards and allow a variety of opportunities to slip right out of our hands, because we think if we don't have money we are worthless. If you believe that, if you think like that, you have been possessed by an evil spirit. You need faith, love and a passionate desire to excise that beast from your being.

I am not lacking the things that really matter.

20 November

Let not what you cannot do tear from your hands
what you can.
– Ashanti proverb

Staying focused on a project or plan is one of the most difficult challenges we face. There is always the house to clean, calls to make, laundry to fold, movies to watch, news to catch up on, deadlines to meet and expectations to live up to. There is so much pulling on us, distracting us, keeping us from doing what we say – no wonder it never gets done. Actually, there is only one thing that keeps us from our goals, that is lack of focus. Very often, lack of focus is caused by fear. Lack of focus/fear means you can find a million reasons not to do what you say you want to do. Lack of focus/fear means if you do what you say you just might succeed. Success means you would move out and beyond your comfort zone. Somehow, somewhere deep inside, that is frightening. The key is if you would just stay focused, all of those frightening little details would miraculously be taken care of. Before you know it, you would be exactly where you say you want to be.

*When I stay focused on the end, the details
are handled.*

Know your friends and then you prosper.
— *The Maxims of Ptahhotpe*

Abundance has absolutely nothing to do with how much money you have. Abundance is about feeling rich and having rich feelings. Abundance is rich relationships, rich experiences, a rich mind and rich ideas that provide you with a sense of meaning. To understand abundance is to create what you want without fear. Abundance is knowing the glass is always half full no matter what is going on. Abundance is feeling good about who you are, where you are and what you have because you realize you don't have to stay there. When your mind is an abundance of ideas, when your hearing is an abundance of love, when your life is an abundance of good people doing good things with you and for you, you are rich beyond words. Abundance begins in mind, extends to the deeds and brings rewards you can bank on even if you cannot put them in the bank.

My abundant source is unlimited.

22 November

I am receptive to the inflow and outpouring of
the universe.
– Eric Butterworth

The world is truly abundant. There are enough trees
to give shade and create oxygen. There is enough grass
to picnic on and feed the worms. There is enough water
to swim in, fish in and feed the animals all over the world.
There is enough sun to shine on everyone. There are
enough animals, plants and minerals to feed everyone and
everything. There truly is enough for us all. We can have
as much as we want if we have faith, courage, determination and perseverance. We are the dealers of our own
hands in life. Our thoughts are the cards we play with.
If we approach life as if we have a full house, we will
reap an abundant jackpot. We must remember that our
experiences can be like baggage. It is a reality, but if we
want to move through life abundantly, we must unpack,
sort out and distribute the baggage to its proper places.
We must talk about what we want, knowing it is in abundance. We must give thanks for universal abundance,
letting the world know we are open and ready to receive
as much goodness as is available.

There is so much abundance for me. I can have it all.

23 November

We must learn to love everyone, everything, everywhere.
– John Randolph Price

Imagine if your job, business or school schedule were a hot new lover you had a lustful interest in. How would you handle it? At the very thought of it you would dress yourself up, sweeten up those secret places and go for it. You wouldn't take 'no' for an answer. You would chase it, pursue it, follow it and find creative ways to get yourself noticed. You would probably fantasize about it, utilizing all your thought sensations. You would imagine how it would feel and smell and even taste if you could just get it to the place you want it. What would you say to it? And how would you want it to see you? Attractive, powerful, successful, in control? And what would you do to your hot new lover once you got your hands on it? Would you stroke it? Fondle it? Caress it? Or would you give it a big crushing embrace while you whispered sweet nothings in his or her ear? Just for today, treat whatever you are doing as if it's a hot new lover. You may find, just for a day, your wildest dream comes true!

I Am in pursuit of a new love.

24 November

Your attitude about who you are and what you have is a very little thing that makes a very big difference.
– Theodore Roosevelt

Can you see, hear and speak? Can you walk, move around and do things for yourself? Did you eat today? Yesterday? Someday last week? Can you pick up a telephone? Turn on a light? Stick a key in a door and have a place to sleep? Are your feet adequately covered? Do you have something to wear? Are your lungs and kidneys functioning? Can you breathe without assistance? Can you move your hands, arms, legs and do the things you want to do? Is there someone who will help you if you need help? Is there someone from whom you receive love? Is there someone you know who will be there no matter what you've done? Can you laugh when you want to? Cry if you need to? Does your mind let you know the difference between the two? Is there a tree you can touch? A flower you can smell? Can you stand in the rays of the sun? Give thanks for every 'yes' you can give and remind yourself that you are truly blessed.

Thank you! Thank you! Thank you! Thank you! Thank you!

25 November

With money a dragon. Without money a worm.
– Chinese proverb

Many people of colour believe that if you have money, you can do any and everything. You cannot. Other people believe that if you don't have money you cannot do anything. They are also wrong. Money is only the visible effect that shows what is going on in your mind. The richer, stronger and clearer your thoughts, the greater your supply of currency. Money doesn't always show up as dollar bills and coins. People you can call on, resources you can draw from, thoughts and attitude – these are also wealth. What you yield in your physical life is the result of how you think. You are your own money. Money is: my own natural energy field. Your thoughts, words, feelings and actions determine your own worth. The quickest way to make money appear is to love yourself, respect yourself and put yourself to work.

I Am money. Money is me.

26 November

When you are employed by God, Inc., you never worry about unemployment.

When you work to obtain greater awareness, knowledge and understanding of yourself, you are working for God. God's goal is for you to be the best you can be with what you have been given and to share what you do with the world. When you do the thing that makes you happy to the best of your ability you are working for God, Inc. The only reason we have come to life in a physical body is to work for and serve the true self within. That is the part of us that is all-wise, all-knowing, all-loving and infinitely creative. When we do what we love, we are happy. When we do what we are good at, we are at peace. When we use what God has given us to create our own work, our rewards do not come from man. Every living person has a desire to do or be something. When you follow that desire, using your gifts, talents and abilities, you can never be out of work.

I Am employed by my God self, which is unlimited.

A man's true wealth is the good he does in the world.
— Mohammed

In many ancient African, Asian and Native American traditions, a person's wealth is measured by the well-being of his or her children. Tradition mandates that you bring children into the world to continue your work and to make additional contributions to the good of the world. If you have no children, your wealth is measured by what you do. Do you sell good products? Do you create good crafts? Do you provide a good service? Do people speak well about you? Do people seek you out to obtain what you have? Do you deal with people honestly? Are you a person of your word? Are you dependable? Reliable? Can you be trusted? Your reputation is your wealth. Your work is a part of your reputation. If you want to pile up riches, give your best to what you do.

I Am my greatest product. I Am my greatest service.

28 November

If a job isn't worth dreaming about, it isn't
worth having.
– Deborah Gregory

You cannot and will not acquire wealth working at a job you do not like. Whatever you spend your life's energy doing, you must be willing to give it your all. The more of yourself you put into your work, the greater it will reward you. We are trained to think in reverse: If you pay me better, I'll work harder. According to the laws of abundance, it doesn't work that way. Your job, work, life assignment must be the spark that fuels your fire. It must be a passion that you pursue. You must want it enough to do it for free. You must be willing to stick with it, taking the ups and downs, giving it all that you are for as long as you can! You've got to taste it, smell it, know it whether you are awake or asleep. If you do not have a lustful passion for your work, you really need to find something else to do.

I Am willing to work at what I love.

Wealth consists not in having great possessions but in
having few wants.
– Epicurus

   You must make yourself content with who you are and
what you have if you want to be truly wealthy.
Contentment does not mean you must stay where you
are; it simply means you have no desperate needs.
Contentment does not mean you cannot want and do
more for yourself; it means you are at peace. The peace
that contentment brings is a quiet peace of mind. With
a peaceful mind you can think and dream; you also get
information about what to do. When your mind is not
filled with desperation and doubt it is primed for inspi-
rational ideas. Our wants rob us of the peace of the
moment; they keep us locked in deprivation and lack.
When we are wanting we are not grateful because we
cannot see what we have. We must learn to be content
in the abundance of where we are if we ever want to
move beyond that spot.

I Am wealthy right here and right now.

30 November

You must begin wherever you are.
– Jack Boland

If you are waiting for something to happen before you begin what you want to do, it will never happen. If you are waiting to get something before you do what you say you want to do, you will never get started. If you are waiting for the right time, the right person, the right circumstances, you could be waiting forever. How about this, what can you do right now? Can you write a letter? Make a call? Finish a plan? Structure a goal? Can you pick a name? Paint a wall? Ask a question? Sweep a floor? Can you structure a schedule? Can you project a date? Can you fulfil a promise? Can you read a book? Can you stop doing all the things you do that keep you from doing the one thing you want to do? Can you pray? Can you sing? Can you dance right where you are? Whatever you can do, you better do it now. Now is all you have to work with.

I Am going to live in the moment.

1 December

It is only through order that greater things are born.
– The Wisdom of the Taoists

There is no way goodness, abundance and success can come to you if your affairs are not in order. The universe is an orderly system of activities and events. Things flow in and out and through. When our home, environment, accounts or activities are not in order, the universal flow will move right past us without stopping. We must recognize and practise divine order if we want ultimate success. We must pay our bills in a timely manner, keeping an organized, structured record of what we pay and when we pay it. Give everyone their due. If we are in debt to someone, pay them. If we cannot pay the agreed upon amount, pay something – and pay it consistently on time. Think of it as giving to God. If we don't give to God, how do we expect God to give back to us? One of the greatest enemies of success is living hand to mouth. Believing we don't have enough, we fail to pay, save and give. In the universal flow, hand to mouth does not work. If we are not living in order we will continue to meet our open mouth with empty hands.

I do have enough to pay, save and give.

2 December

There is a soul force in the universe, which, if we permit it, will flow through us and produce miraculous results.
– Mahatma Gandhi

Each of us on some level tries to elevate ourselves to a new height, a higher standing, a better way of living. Unfortunately, that is why we don't get where we want to be, because we are trying to do it. The power is right where we are. The power is the essence of all that is good. The power is divine. When we believe in the power and seek to make conscious contact with it, the power, not the self, will bring into our lives the very things we are struggling to do. The power will operate in all of our affairs, going before us to prepare our path. The power wants joy, peace, perfect health, abundant wealth and loving relationships for us. The power is the living spirit within buried beneath the personality, ego, perceptions, fears and doubts. The power is the truth of who we are. The power is available; all we have to do is invite it forward and move out of the way.

Today, I Am one with the living spirit who will do the work through me and for me.

3 December

People with ten million dollars are no happier than
people with nine million dollars.
– Hobart Brown

You do not want to be rich and have a diseased body.
You do not want to be healthy and broke. You do not
want to have good health, abundant wealth and poor
relationships. You want to have all of the good. You want
to enjoy every aspect of life abundantly. You want it from
expected and unexpected sources. You want to have more,
give more and get more. In order to do it, you must think
abundantly. Speak abundantly. Do everything in an abundant way. Rest well. Dress well. Eat well and act right.
You cannot achieve abundance with ugly thoughts, words
and deeds. Abundance is a direct reflection of your preparation to live abundantly. People who are abundant do
not worry about what others are doing. People who
expect abundance do not make themselves content to live
in lack. People who are ready for abundance keep their
heads up, their eyes open and give thanks for everything
they get.

I want it all abundantly prospering me now.

4 December

Life is not a problem. If we live, we live; if we die,
we die; if we suffer, we suffer; it appears that we
are the problem.
– Alan Watts

What is prosperity? A mental state. A functional attitude that draws to you an abundance of every great thing.
How do you get prosperity? Expect it. Always ask for
the highest and the best; never doubt that it will come.
What does prosperity look like? Look in the mirror. You
are prosperity. Prosperity is your birthright. It is up to
you to recognize your free access to an inexhaustible supply
of all things good and desirable. You were born into prosperity. It is your inheritance as a child of the kingdom,
a child of the universe. You have been given a body capable
of doing almost anything. It is up to you to convince
your mind that you can. You have been given power,
dominion and authority over everything in the world. It
is up to you how you use it.

When I look at me, I am looking at prosperity.

5 December

Are you one of the human beings who knows there is more to being human than paying bills and not paying bills?
– Rev. Frederick Price

Go ahead, take a moment to pinch yourself. Go ahead, pinch yourself. Feel that? You are alive. You have another opportunity to get this thing together. If you have it together, you have more opportunities for keeping and demonstrating how good you are. Go ahead, pinch yourself again. You have not been carted off to the cemetery. They have not thrown dirt in your face. You can still feel the snow on your face, the rain on your head and the fire under your bottom. You are alive. That is really all it takes. A little time, the opportunity and the desire. If you want abundance, pinch yourself. If you want success, pinch yourself. If you want good loving relationships, pinch yourself. If you really want something good in your life, stop pinching yourself and go out and get it.

All it takes is a little life.

6 December

We don't have to be at the bottom. We were born to
be at the top.
– The Thunder Brothers

Do you know people who say, 'I don't want a lot of
money'? They seem to think if they have a lot of money,
people will want things from them. If they have a lot of
money, they should be willing to share. What about those
people who claim 'Money isn't everything.' They are
right; money isn't everything, but if you don't have it,
you won't have anything. Have you heard, 'Money causes
trouble.' Don't believe it. It is what people do with money,
do for money, do because they don't have money that
causes the problem – not the money. What about, 'I can't
seem to hold on to money.' You shouldn't hold on to
money. You must keep it in the flow, use it wisely, spend
it freely, give and share it lovingly. Money has a face. It
has eyes and ears. If you are not careful about what you
say about money, it has a way of staying away from you.

Money is all right with me.

Act the way you want to be and soon you will be the
way you act.
– Dr Johnnie Coleman

The next time someone says, 'How are you?', try this
answer on for size: I am whole. I am complete. I am
perfect. I am happy. I am dynamite. I am lovable, loving,
getting lots of good love. I am well off and doing well.
I have it all together. I am basking in the riches of life. I
am prospering right here and right now. I am being richly
rewarded, even in my sleep. I am a miracle worker
expecting a miracle right now. I am peacefully peaceful.
I am walking the walk. I am talking the talk. I am claiming
the victory right now. I am successful. I am wealthy. I am
living by pure grace. I am a believer. I am standing on
faith. I am on my way to the top. I am what I am because
I just can't help myself. And how are you doing, my dear?

As I speak it, I Am it.

8 December

NOTICE TO GUESTS: If there is anything you need and don't see, please let us know, we will show you how to do without it.
– Mary McWilliams Fadden

How many times have you let an opportunity go by because you thought you were not prepared? If you sit there waiting for something to happen, when it happens over here, you will be sitting there. If there is something you think will make you better off than you are right now, go find it. See the challenges, face the obstacles, pick up the stumbling blocks, test the waters and imagine the very best that could possibly happen in every situation. It is only when you allow yourself to dream, to see, to feel what you want that it will ever come into existence. Everything happens twice. First on the inside, then on the outside. You must create what you want inside of your heart and mind before you can hope to see it in your world. You cannot build the life you want based on outside stimuli. If it is not in your world, that is because you have not created it. So what in the world are you waiting for?

There is a world inside me waiting to happen.

9 December

You don't need anything to experience prosperity.
– Dwayne Dyer

You might feel that money will make life more simple.
You can begin designing a simpler life right now, without
money, by developing such qualities as inner peace and
becoming more organized in your life. Whatever you feel
money is going to bring, you can begin to feel those qualities within yourself right now and radiate those qualities outward through your thoughts, words and actions.
Rich feelings draw rich experiences. As you think, the
very substance of the universe creates the set of circumstances to bring forth the experience. Thinking and feeling
go hand in hand. Thinking is the masculine faculty within
us all, feeling is the feminine faculty. When you integrate
your thinking and feeling you have a marriage that will
produce children – ideas. With an idea you have an opportunity to create for yourself the exact thing you desire.
Begin, today, to think and feel your good into existence.

All that I want I have right now.

10 December

You survived 100,000 other sperm to get here. What
do you mean you don't know what to do?
– Les Brown

The best-laid plans and strategies are useless unless you
expect to win. And you must know you are going to win
before you start. When you know you are going to win,
you can prepare your victory speech and what you will
wear to the awards dinner the day before it is announced.
When you are a winner, you learn how to take a win no
matter how it comes – whether by default, an interception,
a fumble or when it comes right to you through the air.
Never let a win catch you unexpectedly. Take your wins
in stride. Know they are an everyday occurrence for you
because you expect to win from the beginning. Never let
words of doubt or fear cross your mind; they are the only
things that can steal your win. Win big. Win small. Win
it for yourself. Win it for others. Know what a win will
look like for you, and when it comes, chalk it up to life.

I Am the winning kind.

11 December

A sequential chain of events called growth will bring
forth the fruits of the seeds.
– Rev. Joe Hill

A good farmer does not worry about the weather. He
plants his seeds well, takes great care to till his soil and
knows the seeds will produce. A good farmer does not
plant when the winds are blowing; he waits until there
is peace and calm. He then carefully digs the holes and
places the seeds down with love and prayer. You are a
farmer. Your thoughts are the seeds you plant; they are
the cause of every condition in your life. Your success,
health, wealth and all of your relationships are the fruits
of the seeds you have planted. If you want an abundant
harvest and healthy fruits you must carefully turn the soil
of your consciousness. Get rid of the weeds of doubt,
fear, criticism and judgment of yourself and others. Clear
your mindfield of the rocky areas; whining, complaining
and blaming other farmers for spoiling your crop. Plant
every thought with care and prayer if you want a vast
harvest of healthy crops.

Today I am planting a mindfield of goodness.

We don't know how to celebrate because we don't
know what to celebrate.
– Peter Brock

Guess what? We are having a party today in celebration of you. You are one of your favourite people in the world. You are what life is all about and you know it. So let's celebrate. Let your hair down! Kick off your shoes! Open the windows, the curtains and the blinds! Pump up the volume and let's do it for you! Let's celebrate your victories big and small. Let's celebrate the things you did that you thought you couldn't do, but you did them anyway – and they worked. Let's celebrate because millions didn't make it and you were one of the one's who did. We're going to invite everyone in the world to celebrate in the being of you. We're going to have a lowdown get-down in honour of you. This is what life is all about. Living, laughing and loving; not worrying, working and whining. So come on, get loose, get free, get up so we can get down in celebration of you – let's boogie!

Today is my day to let the good times roll.

13 December

Go and open the mansion of the soul; when you find
the powers of heaven, you shall sit with them.
– *The Book of Coming Forth by Day*, translated by
Dr Maulana Karenga

Where your treasure is there your heart shall be. Your
heart is a place of silence and communion. Your heart
houses the secrets of your soul; the path of your destiny.
Your heart covets your desires and places them strongly
in your mind. It is the key of all you want to be. You
must have faith in your heart and trust all that it says to
you. Never betray your own heart or you will find yourself lost. Your heart is the gatekeeper to your soul. It will
never judge you, never doubt you, for your heart knows
exactly who you are. Keep your heart light from grief.
Let it guide you in all your ways. When things are not
as you know they should be, retreat quietly to the resources
of your heart. You make your heart a mystery. You fail
to ask its advice. When your heart is heavy about a
matter, you believe others can lift you up. If you really
knew your heart you would never doubt its value to you.
God speaks to us through our hearts because all that God
is, is love.

God is in the midst of me. Wherever I Am, God is.

14 December

Talk plenty. Think plenty. Give plenty thanks.
  – Rev. Joe Hill

Open your closet. Do you see shoes, sweaters, pants, dresses? Now, remind yourself you have plenty. Look out of the window. Do you see a tree? Grass? The sky? Now, remind yourself you have plenty. Look at a child. Look at the children, the ideas yet to come, the experiences to be had, the things that must be learned. Now, remind yourself you have plenty. Look at the sun, the moon, the ocean, the stars. Think of the summer, the winter, the spring, the fall. Now remind yourself you have plenty. Turn on the water in the sink. It comes whether you say thank you or not. Now, remind yourself you have plenty. Take a look at the newspaper and ask how many trees it took to make it. Now, remind yourself you have plenty. Think of your heart, lungs, kidneys and liver. Now, remind yourself you have plenty. Remember that the computer is an attempt to re-create the human mind. You have a mind. Now isn't that plenty?

I Am enough. I have enough.

15 December

Success is a journey, not a destination.
– Ben Sweetland

Ernest and Julio Gallo have told us for many years, 'We will sell no wine before its time.' Life treats us much the same way. We are attached to making it quickly. We want everything right now. We make plans and schedule what we want and how it will come. When things do not go our way, we consider it a failure. No matter how hard you push or insist or demand, everything happens when it is supposed to happen; everything comes in time. We really are not in control of the universe, it is so much bigger than we are. Our ego tells us to take control of our time, but what we really do is create confusion and stress. We cannot rush our victory; we cannot cut short our pains. Everything happens when it needs to happen; everyone is always where they need to be. You will never miss out on what is meant for you, even if it has to come to you in a roundabout way. When we relax and follow our inner guidance, everything we should have is all that we get. When we rush around trying to make it, disappointment may be all we get.

I have the time to take my time.

16 December

All you have to do to receive you divine inheritance is
change your old way of thinking.
– John Randolph Price

There is this thing going around. If you are not careful
it will attach itself to you. When it does, it will drain you
of everything you have. It will suck you dry and leave
you to die. This thing is called the Spirit of the Do-Do.
It attacks your brain. It can drive you insane. It never
lets you rest. It is constantly telling you what to do. Do
this! Do that! Do it faster! Do it better! Do it quick! Do
it now! Do it today! Do it for me! Do it for money! Do
it or else! Do it again! You better do it! You better not
do it! They saw you do it! You should do it! You should
not try to do it! When will you do it? How will you do
it? Why would you want to do it? You can't do it! You'd
better do it! Don't you ever do it! There is only one way
to rid yourself of the Spirit of the Do-Do. Close your
eyes, take a deep breath and repeat one hundred times:

Father/Mother Source, what would you have me do?

I can't afford to go around saying it's hard for me because I'm a woman.
– Brig. Gen. Marcelite J. Harris

You know by now that what you focus your mind upon grows. This is key for women. Women do not have it any more difficult than anyone else. It is a matter of what they believe. Women must move into a deeper understanding of their own creative powers. Women create, men direct. Women are the co-creators with the God force; they can manifest life. Women bring to life what is planted through the nurturing power of love. If women want success, prosperity, health or good relations in their lives, they must learn how to make them manifest. Not pushing, forcing, demanding they come. Rather move into your sacred place and space; use your mind's eye, nurture and love yourself and everyone else and let the power of love flow through you.

Today I will love myself healthy and wealthy.

18 December

Giving and receiving are one in truth.
— *A Course in Miracles*

There is only one mind. The mind of the Creator. Each living being is an idea in Divine Mind. We are not separate, as it seems. We are linked through the mighty power of breath. Since we are one, you cannot give anything away; you can only give to yourself. Whatever you give, whatever you do, you are giving and doing to an expression of the one Mind. If you give good, you will receive good. If you do harm, you will feel its effects. If we understand the concept of Divine Mind, we know there is no such thing as stealing from anyone. You can only take away from yourself. Whether the guilt, shame or fear cause the pain, you will take away from yourself that which you believe you are taking from another. When you give, you receive. When you receive it is a reflection of what you give. Since we are all one in Divine Mind, we should make a commitment to always give the best.

Today I will give lovingly and freely to myself.

19 December

I wish I knew how customs got started, it would make
it easier to stamp them out.
– Martin Lane

Right now, in the midst of a so-called recession, many
people are still able to, and do, demonstrate wealth and
abundance. These individuals have overcome the dominant thoughts and beliefs of the mass consciousness that
money is in short supply. Unfortunately, many people still
believe they can't live day to day; they won't make it
through the week; they can't make ends meet; they don't
know what to do to get some of the shrinking money
supply. Many people who believe this way are people of
colour. We have been duped into believing we will never
be self-supporting, self-sufficient, capable of standing on
our own. We are dependent on the system to get better,
give us a break, take care of us. Many of us still believe
the system can and will provide the economic healing we
need – *Until today*! Now hear this, *God does not have
a money problem*! Everything God made is self-sufficient,
including you. If you want to know what to do about
money, ask God.

Dear God, thank you for providing my every need.

20 December

Money was exactly like sex, you thought of nothing
else if you didn't have it and thought of other things
when you did.
– James Baldwin

Every day, our five senses deliver millions of messages
to our brains. We do not remember the messages because
they are filtered through the conscious mind into the
unconscious mind. They are filtered, they are not gone
and they, the unconscious thoughts, govern our attitudes
and behaviours. I need some money . . . Everybody is
broke . . . Money is tight . . . Prices are too high . . . Cut
spending . . . The messages we receive stagnate our abundance consciousness. It is very difficult to think and feel
prosperity when the appearance of lack and limitation is
swallowing us at every turn. Yet until we change our
minds about what we are hearing and thinking, we will
continue to be money miserable. Create the pictures of
what you want in your mind. See your life the way you
want it to be. Write the cheques and envelopes for the
bills before payday. When you are in the company of
money-miserable people, let them know that lack is not
your issue.

Prosperity is my state of mind.

21 December

I like work, it fascinates me, I can sit and look
at it for hours.
– Jerome K. Jerome

Most of us do not work because we want to; we work
because we think we have to work for money. The problem
is that is all we do. We forget that life is more than work.
Life is also about balance. In order to have balance, we
must do more than work. What about fun? We need fun
to keep our minds off work. How about rest? Not just
sleeping to get ready for the next day's work, but resting
the mind and body from all activity. What about solitude? Take an hour or perhaps a day away from the
hustle and bustle of life and people. It's called a mental-
health break. Let us not forget the mind. Education. It
helps to keep the grey matter upstairs from getting dusty.
Work is necessary but it is not the only thing required to
get ahead. All work and no play may give us a balanced
chequebook, but it can also give us an unbalanced mind.

Today I will rest, relax and have some fun.

If you don't do it excellently, don't do it at all. Because if it's not excellent, it won't be profitable or fun.
– Robert Townsend

It takes about as much time to do something really well as it does to do whatever works. What works is not the best you can do. Excellence is. If you want prosperity, wealth, abundance in every area of your life, do what you do with excellence. Excellence requires a commitment, a force from your soul. Excellence is a power source and a sure way to ensure that your product or service will be in demand. Excellence requires order, the first law of prosperity. When you are committed to excellence you must think orderly, behave orderly, conduct yourself in an orderly manner and perform your tasks in order. Excellence is flexible. It does not get stuck in the right way but uses the best of all ways to get the job done. Excellence is cooperation with nature and the forces that be. When you are committed to excellence, the goal helps to keep you focused, not what everyone or anyone else is doing. Excellence is the way to perfect your skill, create a demand and put dollars in the pocket. Do it with excellence.

I Am committed to excellence in all ways.

There is enough in the world for everyone to have plenty to live on happily at peace and still get along with their neighbours.
– Harry S. Truman

The quickest way to block your in-flow of good is to begrudge someone else what they have. We may somehow believe it is our place and duty to judge what other people do. When they receive or achieve beyond our expectations, we become even more judgmental – and sometimes angry. Is the anger really fear that the person will go away and leave us? Or is it fear there is not enough to go around? There are three principles of prosperity we must observe to ensure we receive our good: (1) Ask for what you want, (2) Give what you want away, (3) Be willing to see someone else get what you want before you do. When we follow these principles, we demonstrate our faith that no matter what we have, there is more than enough to go around.

I behold my good in your good.

Prosperity is living easily and happily in the real world,
whether you have money or not.
– Jerry Gillies

If you have many things you are not free to come and
go in life, you are not prosperous. If you have things to
do and protect that you think others can take away from
you, you are not prosperous. If you are not comfortable
with yourself no matter where you are, you are not prosperous. If you believe others can take your ideas, your
mate, your things, you are not comfortable. Prosperity is
a state of mind. When worry or fear crowd your mind,
you cannot be prosperous. If you know you will eat even
when you don't have a dime, you are prosperous. When
you can love and give all that you have, you are prosperous. When you do what you love without pay or
reward, you are prosperous. When you do what you can
because you can, not for money only, you are prosperous.
When you love all people for who they are, not for what
they can give you, you are a wealthy being. Prosperity is
a state of mind.

The richer I think, the richer I Am.

25 December

Make a prayer acknowledging yourself as a vehicle of
light, giving thanks for all that has come today.
– Dhyani Ywahoo

Just for today, allow yourself to embrace all that you
are every moment. Know that you are a vessel of light.
Allow yourself to release all doubts about your ability,
the mistakes of the past, the fear of the future. Just for
today, remember that you have grace. It is called breath.
You have a connection to the Divine Mind, the power
source of the world. Just for today, remind yourself, 'I
am one with God.' 'I am one with all the power there
is.' Just for today, be a little child. Know the world is
safe. Know that you are loved. Know that just where you
are, God is. Just for today, be free. Be peace-filled. Be
loving to yourself and all others. Know that you shall
not want for any good thing. Just for today, give praise
and thanksgiving for everything to let the universe know
you are ready to receive more.

*Let the light shine on me today. I give
praise and thanks.*

26 December

Let there be everywhere our voices, our eyes, our
thoughts, our love, our actions, breathing hope
and victory.
– Sonia Sanchez

In the twenty-first century the power is with the people.
The people are the force that will make or break the
world as we know it. The people are the only voice that
will matter. The people have the power to create the
world they want to see. The power is their thoughts, their
words, their actions toward one another. Who are the
people? Not the priests, the heads of state, the presidents.
The people are those who can surrender their ego, embrace
themselves as they are and do what they have been sent
to do. The people are those who know they are not in
charge; rather, they give praise to the Creative Source of
life. The people are those who control their breath, know
their bodies and use both to teach others how to do it.
The people are the children. The people are the women.
The people are the elders. The people are the men who
love, nurture and protect the children, women and elders.
The people are the light.

Today I Am a person of power.

In this world it is not what we take up but what we give up that makes us right.
— Henry Beecher

There is a very simple principle that people cannot seem to get the hang of – as you give, so you receive. People find it difficult to believe that it is necessary to give first and give righteously. If you only give to get, you will not receive. If you give out of fear, you will not receive. Many people of colour do not believe they have enough to give. That is because they may be thinking in terms of money only. If you do not have money, give of your time, talent and energy. Give a smile. Give a prayer. Give anonymously without expectation of recognition. The spirit in which you give determines the manner in which you receive. If you give freely, joyously and willingly, you will receive abundantly. As you give what you have, what you are not using, you make room to receive something else in its place. Give of yourself, your knowledge and the information you have received, then prepare yourself for an outpouring of blessing. And by the way, do not expect it to come back to you from the person you gave it to.

Today I lovingly give my all to all who may need.

28 December

Unhappiness is not knowing what we want and killing ourselves to get it.
– Don Harold

Can I continue to live in lack and limitation, denying myself the abundant goodness of the world? Or can I make a plan, follow a dream, do what I can, where I am, with what I have? Can I? Can I? Can I continue to buy into the belief that there is not enough, I am not enough, settling for whatever I can get? Or can I do my best in every situation, expecting the best from every situation, recognizing that what I put out must come back to me tenfold? Can I? Can I? Can I continue to live in fear, complaining about what I do not have, cannot do, criticizing myself and others? Or can I take a chance, find an opportunity and know in my heart what I want to do is possible? Can I? Can I? Can I blame the world, hate my enemy, feel sorry for myself as an excuse not to do what I desire to do? Or can I raise my consciousness, pour love into every situation and take responsibility for myself? Can I? Can I? Can you?

I Am responsible for doing all I can do.

Wealth is not in making money but in making the
person while they make money.
– John Wicker

Do I see anything that needs to be done for me that I
am not doing? Or do I only see what others could be
doing and are not? Do I? Do I? Do I support myself by
nurturing myself, accepting what I feel and letting my
needs be known? Or do I shrink under criticism, blame
others for my conditions and look for the easy way out?
Do I? Do I? Do I recognize my truth and speak it when
I feel the need? Or do I allow fear and people pleasing
to silence me? Do I? Do I? Do I continue to do the things
I know are not good for me and do not bring me what
I want? Or do I examine myself, correct myself, accept
myself but commit to get better? Do I? Do I? Do I know
what I want, believe I can have it, do everything in my
power to bring it about? Or do I accept what others tell
me about my limitations and limit myself to what they
believe? Do I? Do I? Do I have faith in spirit, faith in
myself, faith in things unseen? Do I? Do I? Do you?

I am not what I used to be. I am doing much better.

30 December

If money is your hope for independence, you will
never have it.
– Henry Ford

Will I make it through the difficult times? Or will I
give up? Will I? Will I? Will I get up this morning with
a positive attitude, greet everyone with a smile and be
glad to be alive? Or will I take a bad attitude into the
world and have everyone wish I were not? Will I? Will
I? Will I accept the people I encounter today for who
they are and encourage them to become part of the group?
Or will I seek out the people I feel are superior to the
rest and alienate myself from those I judge beneath me?
Will I? Will I? Will I do my part and give of myself to
create my own independence? Or will I accept the crumbs
that keep me dependent on people, conditions and situations? Will I? Will I? Will I trust myself and follow my
first thought? Or will I look for others to validate me?
Will I? Will I? Will you?

*Today I will know me, honour me, support me and
trust me.*

31 December

Your crown has been bought and paid for. All you
must do is put it on your head.
– James Baldwin

There is nothing you need that you do not already
have. There is nothing you need to know that you do
not already know. There is nothing you want that does
not already exist. There is nothing that exists that is too
good for you. There is nothing anyone has that you
cannot have. There is nothing more powerful, more intelligent, more sacred than you. You are the stuff life is
made of. You are the essence of life. You have been
chosen at this time, in this place to be among the living.
You come from a long line of successful living beings.
You are one of the king's kids. Born into the world to
inherit the kingdom. You are equipped to handle anything.
You live by grace, built by love. You are the cause and
the reason of everything you see. You are one with the
Source. You are creative. You are alive. What else could
possibly matter?

Today I claim my Divine inheritance.

INDEX